Welcome to *Airlock*!

Airlock is a Bible reading guide that contains 13 weeks' worth of undated material. You can use it whenever you like, wherever you like. There are six pages per week – five daily notes and a little extra for the weekend – but feel free to use it in the way that benefits you the most.

Each daily page is divided into three sections:

Decompress

This is a short prayer or thought designed to get you in the right frame of mind to read the Bible, and to prepare you for what you're about to read. After the Decompress section, you'll be given the Bible passage for the day. It doesn't matter what Bible version you use – just make sure you open up your Bible!

Immerse

This section contains ways of relating the Bible passage to today's culture. It also explains anything difficult in the Bible passage, and will help you understand the context the passage was written in.

Re-engage

This section encourages you to take what you've learned from the Bible passage and apply it to your day-to-day life through practical suggestions and pointers.

In this issue, Esther, Micah and Nahum come into view, we get to the end of Matthew, Acts and 2 Corinthians, and continue our journey through the books of Psalms and Isaiah.

Step into the *Airlock* and relieve the pressure!

Written by Andy Brown (H/26–30), Darren Hill (H/06–10, H/41–45), Howard Ingham (H/16–20, H/36–40, H/61–65), Nick Lear (H/21–25), James Lovelock (H/11–15, H/51–55), Anne Phipps (H/01–05), Steve Tilley (H/31–35, H/56–60) and Rachel Wild (H/46–50). Extra material provided by Ro Willoughby.

Designed and illustrated by Martin Lore. Cover photography by Chris Brown.

Theme: Deliverance

The dogs of war

H/01

Decompress

Everybody has something that traps them. It could be feeling hemmed in by exams, worried about a habit, being afraid of somebody... Do you think you're coping OK on your own with it? But wouldn't it be better to be free? Can you really cope alone with being surrounded? Being trapped?

NOW READ PSALM 59

Immerse

This psalm was probably written by David when he was being attacked by Saul (though there may have been additions later). The story in 1 Samuel 19 is fantastic. Saul is concerned that David is so well known and decides the only solution is to kill his rival(!). His son, Jonathan, calms him down with some clever negotiation, but when David is sitting playing his harp one day, Saul suddenly goes bonkers and attacks him with a spear. David dodges and the spear gets stuck in the wall. David realises it's not all that safe round Saul.

>That night, surrounded by his enemies, David's wife lowers him out of the window to save his life. She shoves an idol into bed with her and when the henchmen arrive, she does a pretty good job of stalling ('He's ill! He's ill! OK, so yes, he's not breathing. And he's a lot smaller than he used to be... err... Oh, would you look at that, he's turned into an idol!'), so David can get as far away as possible.

>It's worth looking at the psalm in the light of when it was written. Verses 6,7 and 13,14 powerfully show David's feelings about his attackers, but his trust in God (verses 16,17) overrides everything. Reread the psalm and picture David hiding out, far from home, writing the words in the dark.

Re-engage

There are two things which are repeated in the psalm: one is the idea of snarling dogs and the other is that God is your strength. These are significant for us. Everyone's got their dogs, even if they're puppies rather than Rottweilers. It could be parents applying pressure, friends being better than you at everything, worry about careers or money. Or it could be being afraid of something – driving failing, hedgehogs... But no matter how many dogs you've got snarling at you, God is your strength, and he's so strong that it's worth the psalmist saying it more than once. God is your strength.

>Picture your 'dogs' now and submit each one to God's control.

Airlock: Heavenly

Themes: **Desperation, Triumph**

Bridlington is my washbowl!

Decompress

God is in charge of everything. Picture him as a mighty king, holding the world in one hand. He controls it all, whether the actual globe, or the world in which you live: your family, your friends, your workplace, your college, your church. Speak to him now to thank him for his strength and the fact that you can rely on him.

NOW READ PSALM 60

Immerse

The psalm was probably written after a national disaster – possibly after a battle with Edom (v 9). The king is gutted that God no longer seems to be on his army's side. But the psalmist still trusts in his God. Take a look again at the last few verses. He gets himself into the right frame of mind by focusing on how strong God is. He looks at all the countries surrounding him and points the finger at them, almost laughing, saying, 'See how small you are compared to my God!' With that perspective the psalmist sees how the future might be: a triumph, with God's help even in the most desperate times.

Re-engage

My friend put down the phone, looked at me, and I knew it was bad news. She took a step into the kitchen and didn't even pause before she said it. She didn't want to have this as a secret for more than a second or two. 'James is dead. It was a car accident.' I watched myself as if I was in a film. I stood there for a moment, not saying anything, and then began to turn away because I wanted my face to have some privacy while it worked out how it should look. But my left leg gave out and I staggered into the counter.

> 'You have given your people trouble. You made us unable to walk straight …'

> You may be staggering now, or you may have suffered in the past, or you may never have had the kind of desperate times the psalmist writes about. But one day, when the ground begins to move and the world is torn open, this psalm is the place to come, because God stands over it all solidly, triumphing over tragedy.

> Every problem is small when seen in relation to the God we've got on our side. Make a list of the things that you deal with day to day, and fit them into the words of the psalm: 'Work and church are mine… I throw my sandals at money problems… Bridlington is like my washbowl.'

Airlock: Heavenly

Theme: Refuge

Feel the fear and run away

Decompress

Where do you feel safe? Is there a particular person or place that makes you feel secure, and as if nobody can touch you? If God isn't automatically in that safe place with you, invite him in now. And if you don't feel there's anywhere safe for you in the world, ask God to put his fortress arms round you.

NOW READ PSALM 61

Immerse

My mum was always very keen on me facing my fears. Whether it was walking out on stage, riding a bike or jumping off tall buildings, she told me I HAD to do it and face the fear (well, maybe not with the tall buildings one!).

>But facing your fear isn't always possible. It might just be too hard to face, or maybe facing it would put you in danger. At times like these we want to be carried away to a 'high mountain' (v 2), just to get a break.

>I don't think the high mountain necessarily has to be an actual place. For instance, most of us need a place of safety from our thoughts when they threaten to overwhelm us. When we get depressed or angry or obsessed or freaked out we need to find a way of breaking free of the emotion and finding a place of peace and safety in our minds. In those situations, God can become a fortress against those things in our heads that we can't stand alone. He is the strong tower nothing can conquer; the high mountain we can run away to.

Re-engage

Try to think practically about how God could be your high mountain Are there particular prayers you could say, or Bible passages you can come back to again and again when you're struggling? Finding a quiet spot to give your thoughts and feelings over to God can be massively powerful.

>But this psalm can mean much more too. 'I call to you from the ends of the earth.' Safety for many people is a place where they can be free from the fear of injury and violence, poverty and death: a house or a town they can run to and not be afraid of men with guns or children with machetes. In this psalm, God is that kind of shelter as well – a shelter spiritually, mentally and physically for all the oppressed people in the world. What a God we worship!

Airlock: Heavenly

Themes: **Rest, Perspective**

Protection

Decompress

'Come to me, all of you who are tired and have heavy loads, and I will give you rest. Accept my teachings and learn from me, because I am gentle and humble in spirit, and you will find rest for your lives.'
Matthew 11:28,29

NOW READ PSALM 62

Immerse

The psalmist is an important guy. He's probably one of the most educated and powerful people in the kingdom. But this psalm shows him recognising his real position when looked at it in relation to God. He focuses on what God is like and what God can do rather than saying what he (the writer) can do. In verses 9 and 10 the writer advises us, and reminds himself, to put everything in that framework – God as the everlasting rock and us as no more than an intake of breath.

>In fact there's only one thing we can do which will have any effect (v 8). God does all of the other stuff: saving, protecting and giving rest. These things are so important that they're repeated like a chorus in a song – God saving and defending as the thread running though everything.

Re-engage

It's easy to say that we only find rest in God, but much harder to put that into practice. We actually find rest in lots of ways: by hanging out with friends, snoozing in an armchair, chatting to our family, sitting alone with a good book or having a cold Irn-Bru on a summer's evening. All of those things could be part of finding rest in God, as long as we put him first, but the best way is to focus on God.

>What do we need 'defence' from? What do we need 'rest' from? It could be something really clear like bullying or a difficult situation. But it could also be something less obvious, like our own thoughts or behaviour. In those cases, we could actually be running away from the problem by blanking it out (with friends or family or Irn-Bru) and real rest can only be found by telling it to God and letting him worry about it, rather than hugging it to ourselves.

Airlock: Heavenly

Themes: **Desires, Needs**

Obey your thirst

Decompress

What would you say are the things you need? Food and shelter obviously, but there's so much more. Ask God for these things. Add in the things that you want. And don't be afraid to ask for the ones that aren't all 'holy'.

NOW READ PSALM 63

Immerse

The person writing the psalm has a desperate need for God. He associates his need for God with very physical desires: food, drink, sleep. There's no separation between his physical needs and his powerful desire for God. It's all tied up in the same thing.

> It's only in the second half of the psalm that you realise he actually has a very pressing and scary need. People are trying to bump him off. But instead of starting the psalm with, 'Er... God, I need to be rescued and be safe,' he's started it with, 'I need you, I need you, I need you!' It's hard to put our immediate needs to one side, but that's what God sometimes asks us to do in prayer. Crave God first and ask for your other desires knowing they'll never be as important as knowing him.

Re-engage

I had the crummiest job in the whole youth hostel. I was balancing on a tall ladder painting the side of the hostel bright white to entice other poor backpackers in. It had seemed like a fun job for the first, oh, 40 seconds or so, but by the 42nd or 43rd second my arms were aching, the smell of the paint was drying my mouth and nose and the sun was beating on the back of my head with the power of a microwave (though I hope my brains weren't being cooked inside out). The worst of it was, I had to stay up there as long as possible, as coming down was such a palaver. I began to fantasise about cool shade and a milkshake; after a few more minutes it was a cold shower and a lemonade. But as the minutes dragged out, everything was purged from my mind except, 'When can I get a glass of water?' was practically hallucinating. Water was all that mattered. I didn't mind if it was lukewarm or a bit cloudy. I just craved water.

> I don't think I've ever craved God like that. Do you want to put yourself in that position? Do you want to crave God that badly, so that the only way you can see yourself satisfied is by knowing him better?

Airlock: Heavenly

Crooked Eric's protection racket

'Ere. If you pay up a pony a week, then your "Cockney Pie and Mash Emporium" will be as safe as houses. But if you don't, then I'll send the lads around and there'll be more than 'taters that'll be mashed, get what I'm sayin', me old china? Ha, ha, ha!'

God's protection racket

'I love you, LORD.
    You are my strength.
The LORD is my rock,
    my protection, my Saviour.
My God is my rock.
I can run to him for safety.
He is my shield and my saving strength, my defender.'
Psalm 18:1,2

God's love and protection is unconditional, not dependent on us doing stuff for him or paying him a pony, a monkey or any other Cockney-rhyming animal. Your life won't be perfect, but God will always be there for you. He won't turn against you if you don't give him the right payment. If you have anything you want to ask him, any troubles you find yourself in, then talk to him.

Extra 1_2 Samuel 22
Extra 2_Proverbs 3

Themes: God's Word, Judgement

Here comes the judge

Decompress

Who are you? Take a moment to think of who you are: an individual, part of a group of friends, part of a community, a town, a city, a nation!

NOW READ MICAH 1

Immerse

Micah is the type of guy we'd probably feel for big time if he were around today. He was not one of the regular prophets from the big city, and not from a connected family – the text would give his father's name if he were. So he was probably a bit of an underdog; but as the passage says, he spoke God's word for many years. The list of kings given in the passage show that his propheteering may have gone on for almost half a century. Unfortunately his words weren't quite so uplifting for the people of Israel and Judah. By this time Israel was two nations, with two capitals – Samaria and Jerusalem – and Micah's prophecy looks towards the time when both Israel and Judah are going to be conquered and the nations effectively will no longer exist.

>We get so much legal language here, it's like an episode of Judge John Deed, but instead of boring courtrooms we have the wonderful imagery of what happens when the judge comes to town: the mountains melting and so on.

>In verse 5, the capital cities are blamed for the sins of the nations. This shows vividly that the people of God are seen as a whole. The sin is passed from the capitals to the outlying reaches of the land. This is often the way things spread: what is big in the capital doesn't take long to move out to the countryside; and in our ever-shrinking world, things that go on in other countries can now spread easily over cyber-borders.

Re-engage

How often do we try to blame a 'part' of ourselves that is not directly under our control when we do something wrong? 'Oh, I can't help that, it's because of my personality.' And it is not just us as individuals. Do we stand shoulder to shoulder with others in our community when there is something wrong, or do we try to stand to one side, exempting ourselves from blame? If something is wrong in our society we have to make a stand, we have to be the voice of God, when all around us are shouting their own words.

Airlock: Heavenly

Theme: Social justice

Because I can

Decompress

In the space below, take a few moments and list the greatest evils of our age. What are the things that upset you most about our world?

Look at your list and see how many of those evils are created by humanity.

NOW READ MICAH 2

Immerse

The situation is quite bad here. Those who are in power seem to be a nasty lot – there is a list of bad things that they get up to, from the moment they wake up in fact, and that isn't just saying that they aren't morning people. The leaders of the country were treating those with less than themselves in a disgusting way. They were taking what wasn't theirs, so that those with little ended up with even less – sound familiar?

>Some things cannot be stopped. The wounds here can't be healed and eventually they are going to be fatal for both the country and those causing the trouble. They will lose all that they have taken from others and destruction is looming.

>But the bigger picture shows that there is hope in the long run for the nation. Eventually they will be led out of exile. However, when that happens it will be the Lord who is leading them, not the corrupt rulers and people in power that they currently have.

Re-engage

The people don't believe God could do such a thing. They were trying to tell Micah to keep quiet and stop being such a doom merchant. They were in their land, promised by God; he wouldn't let them be defeated and taken off elsewhere, would he?

>What do others, and possibly we ourselves, believe God wouldn't do today? I mean, he is a God of love, isn't he? He wouldn't punish people for not believing in him, or for not following him, would he? Do we want a God who only tells us good things and lets us get on with enjoying our lives without any consequences? Don't we have a duty to follow God and to help those who are being oppressed?

Airlock: Heavenly

Theme: Guidance

I can't hear you

Decompress

Imagine nothing! Go on have a go: silence, no sound, no sight, no smell, no communication at all...
>It's called sensory depravation and it eventually turns you quite mad: look at the Chuckle Brothers.

NOW READ MICAH 3

Immerse

The leaders of Israel were a bad bunch, as we saw in chapter 2, but Micah has not finished. As leaders they have a duty to look after their people but they haven't been doing it. Organised religion was the big thing at this time. The leaders looked to the prophets, often paid prophets, to tell them what they should do. Officially this was God's will but often they would say just what the leaders wanted to hear. But God is going to change all that. God will no longer talk to the prophets, God will go silent and not answer any calls for guidance because of their lies in the past.
>For a nation relying on organised religion to guide it this would be a disaster. It's like a newspaper losing contact with its journalists, or a computer losing contact with the Internet. Not only would there be sensory depravation, but the whole set-up would be undermined, if it were not for Micah. He is the one who will be able to pass on God's words, but they won't be the sort the nation is hoping for. Again Micah is talking about the destruction of Jerusalem the home of the organised religion the home of the temple – the capital city of God's people.

Re-engage

How do you view the leaders of your country? It is very easy to criticise them and moan from our safe houses, but could or should we be doing a little more to help them treat their countries with respect and justice?
>If we see something unjust going on, we can do things about it. The great thing about democracies is that we have a say. In a country where free speech is allowed we can join pressure groups to fight against injustices. The pressure being put on the rich nations to help poorer nations has come from people like you and me. We can have a voice and not just in this way: we shouldn't forget the power of prayer when it comes to sorting out the leaders of our countries. Why not spend a little time in prayer, asking God to guide your leaders in the decisions they have to make? You have a voice, make it count!

Airlock: Heavenly

Themes: **Justice, Exile**

In exile

Decompress

If things are going badly, what do you do? Do you sit and wallow in despair, complaining that life isn't fair? Do you just accept what is happening?

>Or do you learn from your situation, pick yourself up and face the future, trusting that God will see you right in the end?

NOW READ MICAH 4

Immerse

Micah goes on to say that one day things will be different. One day God's words will go further. We have heard that the leaders have caused pain for the people of the nation, but here Micah tells them what things will be like in the future.

>It is quite interesting that Micah talks about how war will be turned to peace. Many African nations are currently struggling in poverty because they have been at war for many years; they are struggling with debt because they have had to buy arms to fight with while the people have starved; they may have kept their borders safe but their people have gone hungry and now they can't afford to feed them.

>But this chapter deals with the future. The nation will be punished in the short-term, but as history unfolds there will be a glorious future for those who follow God: he will again lead his people, from his holy city.

Re-engage

Where are we today? In the Western world the church is in a state of decay. The number of people who attend churches is falling and the church seems to have little voice in the world. Being a Christian is seen as being a bit old hat, and although we aren't persecuted for what we believe it is rare that our opinions are taken seriously.

>I have heard it said several times that the church, especially in the United Kingdom, might be in a state of exile, just like God's people were after Micah's prophecy. If this is so, then what will happen? We can only pray and learn from what is happening now. If we are in exile then we can only grow closer to God. This will lead us to become better followers: if we believe and trust in God it will develop our character. Then one day, we too may be able to return to our true home, with God as our leader, for all the nations to see.

Airlock: Heavenly

Theme: **The Messiah**

Future perfect

Decompress

Take a moment to think about one thing, the removal of which would cause society to fall apart. Any ideas? What if we lost electricity, or the power to use computers? What if we lost the very society that we live in?

NOW READ MICAH 5

Immerse

Micah now contrasts two things. The first is the current king and leaders of the nation. The city is going to be captured and the leaders are going to be attacked. History tells us that they were deposed and carried away into exile. The society that God's people had enjoyed for so long was going to be torn asunder, and completely fall apart.

>The second is the future king, and boy what a king that will be. Here is one of the Old Testament references to the Messiah, God's chosen one, the Christ. Micah is talking about Jesus. Over 700 years before a baby boy is born in Bethlehem, Micah is talking about him. This is the reference to which Herod's advisers turn when asked where the Messiah will be born.

>Then Micah is back talking about the people who are left after the exile. God won't let them be exiled forever, and when that exile is over he will tear down all the false gods from Assyria, and eventually everyone will know that Yahweh is God.

Re-engage

Micah talks about all the possessions and idols that the Assyrians used in their conquering and worship in verses 10–14. The nation of Assyria was proud in all that it had achieved and it believed its army was invincible. But Micah points out that everything they had, from possessions to idols, was all man-made: made in their own image. And because they were man-made they could be destroyed – they would not last forever.

>We need to place our faith firmly in our God. Our God isn't man-made; in fact we are made in his image as we are told in Genesis. Spend some time praying to our Lord and Saviour, Jesus, the Messiah, God's chosen one. Chosen to lead us both now and in our life to come. Ask for strength to focus on him and not on things that we make, and for power to not let anything of this world come between us and his love.

Airlock: Heavenly

OK, so it may not be Christmas when you're reading this, but the fact that Micah predicted Jesus' birth certainly makes you think. Well before Micah's time, God's great salvation plan was in place, and it wasn't just Micah who foretold the coming of Jesus.

What does it mean to you that God's plan for salvation is in action?

How does it make you feel that God has a plan for your life?

Do you know what God has in store for you?

Extra 1_Isaiah 9:1–7
Extra 2_John 1:1–18

Theme: Weakness

Peter imperfect

Decompress

'The law that brought death was written in words on stone. It came with God's glory, which made Moses' face so bright that the Israelites could not continue to look at it. But that glory later disappeared.'
2 Corinthians 3:7

NOW READ MATTHEW 26:69–75

Immerse

It's lucky that this story wasn't set in the modern days of media hype. You can just imagine Peter's media guru having a long discussion with Matthew about re-editing this little scene, because it hardly makes the founder of the church look like the swashbuckling, heroic man of Christ that we expect.

>But this is exactly the point. Peter was a passionate, headstrong and emotional man who thought with his instinct, not his intellect. When he was confronted with the pressures of being associated with a 'criminal', he instinctively set out to protect himself by lying. The thing is that Jesus knew him well enough to know exactly what would happen even before he entered the courtyard (26:31–35).

>Yes, Peter was passionate, presumptuous and proud, but one 'p' he was not was 'perfect'. And God chose this moment to humble him – to show him his limitations and prepare him for the tasks ahead. This would not be the last time that Peter got it wrong (see his disagreements with Paul in Acts!), but Peter learned a lot about the differences between thoughts, words and actions that day…

Re-engage

Have you ever wondered about what would have happened if Peter hadn't lied? Would he have been arrested? Crucified too?

>God had incorporated Peter's weakness into the plan for his church. Peter had all the best intentions about standing up for Jesus, but his courage let him down at the last minute. But it didn't matter. Peter felt terrible when Jesus was proved right, but the fact that he was a liar didn't stop God from using him in the future (indeed, if you read John 21:15–19, you will see a rather formal forgiveness of Peter).

>Now, I am not saying that you shouldn't care about your mistakes. Peter did care. But when we do get things wrong – and we will – we should remember that even the best of disciples screwed up sometimes. God has a knack of using weaknesses and mistakes…

Airlock: Heavenly

Theme: Greed

Planning with the enemy

Decompress

'No one who trusts you (God) will be disgraced, but those who sin without excuse will be disgraced.' Psalm 25:3

NOW READ MATTHEW 27:1–10

Immerse

Some years ago, I remember having an argument with my youth leader about whether Judas would go to heaven. In my best smarmy voice, I argued: 'Yes, but Judas was part of God's plan, so he must have therefore been following God's will, so he must be going to heaven, so NER NER NER.'

>Why is it that Peter was forgiven for denying Jesus, but Judas chose to destroy himself? I believe the answer is in one of the words I used yesterday – intentions. Judas' motive for betraying Jesus was greed: he did it for the money.

>Sometimes it was argued that as Judas was a Zealot – part of a religious sect that believed the Messiah would overthrow the Romans and restore the Jews to their rightful place – he was frustrated by the fact that Jesus never looked like doing this. However, the fact that he betrayed Jesus for money suggests that it was a selfish motive rather than for the good of anyone else.

>But God knew exactly how Judas would behave even before he met with the Pharisees. And once again, Judas' act of treachery that should have ended God's plan was incorporated to move it on to its next stage.

>Only God knows whether Judas repented before he died, or whether God showed him forgiveness. But, it proves that God is in control above any evil-doing; nothing can stop his master plan.

Re-engage

The world is a scary place today. I am writing these notes just after the London bombings in July 2005, and once again we are living in a time of fear and uncertainty.

>And yet I know that God is still working his plan out, despite the greed, confusion and evil in the world. Even through the darkest valley, God can shine a light – and once his light shines even in the tiniest way, the darkness is no longer complete.

>God will never, ever allow any human error to sidetrack his plan for you and all of his children. Never be afraid if your hope is in God, because you will never, ever be put to shame.

Airlock: Heavenly

Theme: Leadership

Pilate the librarian

Decompress

'If your fellow believer sins against you, go and tell him in private what he did wrong. If he listens to you, you have helped that person to be your brother or sister again.'
Matthew 18:15

NOW READ MATTHEW 27:11–14

Immerse

Poor old Pilate. He's not the sharpest tool in the tool-box, is he? And unfortunately, his high position seems to have turned him into a 'helpful old librarian' character rather than giving him real leadership skills.

>To be fair, Pilate does cotton on to the fact that this is a set-up quite early on. But unfortunately, he seems to treat Jesus rather like a batty old lady who is trying to check her sandwiches out at the book issuing desk.

>'Now Jesus, do you UNDERSTAND what they're SAYING? They're SAYING you've been VERY NAUGHTY about the JEWISH LEADERS. Now if you just say SORRY, I'm sure we can get this SORTED OUT NICELY. OK?'

>It doesn't take much to work out that Pilate is in the wrong job. He is a weak leader who is swayed by people's opinion. But guess what? God knew this, and he incorporated it into his plan.

Re-engage

The world is full of people who will do anything for a quiet life, and I have to admit that I'm sometimes one of them. It's the occasions when you can see someone heading down the wrong path, but you don't tell them in case you upset them. Or the times when you agree with something at school or at work, even though your heart is telling you that it's not the right direction. Or when you've got a gift that your church could use, but you hide it in case you upset other people by looking too keen or too talented.

>Apathy is one of the main enemies of the church today. It is no good being a nice old librarian; sometimes we need to get a little bit more assertive and forceful. We need to look after each other, and that sometimes means being unpopular by voicing a particular viewpoint.

>We need to keep praying things through, and if you hear God speaking – let other people know!

Airlock: Heavenly

Theme: **Leadership**

Mr Popularity

Decompress

'Brothers and sisters, I ask you to look out for those who cause people to be against each other and who upset to other people's faith. They are against the true teaching you learned, so stay away from them. Such people are not serving our Lord Christ but are only doing what pleases themselves. They use fancy talk and fine words to fool the minds of those who do not know about evil.' Romans 16:17,18

NOW READ MATTHEW 27:15–26

Immerse

You have to feel a little sorry for the buffoon that is Pilate. The ultimate politician: his only worry is whether he's doing enough to keep people happy and get himself re-elected.

>Having said this, the whole Jesus and Barabbas thing is a pretty quick-thinking idea to get Jesus off the hook. But Pilate has reckoned without the interference of the Jewish leaders.

>Remember that the Jewish leaders are hostile to the possibility that Jesus is their Messiah – as Jesus says, 'though hearing they do not hear'. The leaders are adamant that Jesus must be killed for the sake of their religion, from which Jesus is turning the people away.

>The Jewish leaders' weakness is their blindness; but do you know, God has predicted this, and incorporated it into his plan. Jesus must die – but not for the reasons that the Pharisees expect…

Re-engage

Pilate is a good example of a weak leader – he knows what is right, but allows popular opinion to change his mind. Pilate may have washed his hands of Jesus, but it did not absolve him from the fact that he failed to act on his own instincts.

>Being a leader is difficult, especially since we are human beings who make mistakes. Recent leaders have made a big deal about 'listening to the people', which is all well and good, but if the government really did what people wanted, there would be an awful lot of people sitting watching re-runs of Coronation Street and munching pizzas (or is it just me?).

>Don't get me wrong, I'm not saying that leaders shouldn't listen to their people, but one of the main qualities of leadership is having convictions and sticking to them. The Bible is our guidebook, and if we are in a position of leading others, we should not be afraid to guide people despite the fact that it might make us unpopular.

Airlock: Heavenly

Theme: Bullying

Humiliating the Samaritan

Decompress

'As a man was going down from Jerusalem to Jericho, some robbers attacked him. They tore off his clothes, beat him, and left him lying there, almost dead.'
Luke 10:30

NOW READ MATTHEW 27:27–31

Immerse

I find this one of the most shocking passages in the Bible – even more so because it has so many resonances with the present day. It shows the bully-boy mentality that we read about in the newspapers so often today, where an individual is picked on for being different.

>You only have to think about the reported prisoner abuse in the Iraq war, or the torture that some regimes inflict on people of different religions or cultures, or even incidents where the town 'chav' gang attacks an individual 'goth' (or indeed vice versa).

>That this should happen to Jesus is doubly shocking. Jesus was the man who dined with prisoners and spoke to prostitutes – the man who sought to unite the poor and the weak. And yet he took this kind of treatment without any resistance.

>I can't imagine what was going through Jesus' mind as he was mocked, humiliated and physically damaged by the people he was about to die for. But even through writing this note, it has become clearer to me why we have times of praise and worship to Jesus: he certainly was an amazing man.

Re-engage

Reading this passage reminded me of 'The good Samaritan' – but without the Samaritan. Jesus is beaten, kicked and robbed of his dignity – but there is no one there to save him, or take him to safety.

>I have often identified with the man that gets attacked in 'The good Samaritan' – and have sometimes aspired to be the Samaritan himself. And I know there have been times when I have walked past like the Priest or the Levite. But this passage gives me the feeling that I have sometimes even behaved like the robbers.

>It is so easy to get sucked into 'ganging up' on someone, because they're different, or for some other reason. But although Jesus is on the lookout for the good Samaritan, he also identifies very strongly with the man on the road, because he's been there. I pray that we will be on the looking out for lonely travellers – but to help them rather than hurt them…

Airlock: Heavenly

Extra H/11–15

A quiz for your enjoyment

1 If you could only save one thing from your house, before it was eaten by a giant goat, what would it be?
a) Photographs of you puking up on the Nemesis at Alton Towers
b) Your favourite teddy bear
c) Your complete collection of Beano comics
d) Something else

2 If you had to give up something for Lent, what would be the hardest thing to go without?
a) Chocolate
b) Watching T4
c) Listening to Barry Manilow
d) Something else

3 If by giving up your life, you could save the lives of 20 other people, what would you do?

Jesus' actions were the ultimate sacrifice. It is hard even to begin to understand what he did for us, so that we could be saved. Spend some time in quiet, trying to grasp hold of a little bit of what that means. It might help to read one of the other accounts of Jesus' sacrifice.

Extra 1_Luke 22,23
Extra 2_John 18,19

Themes: **Persecution, Solutions**

Trouble

Decompress

If you lived in a country where Christianity was illegal and you saw someone being beaten up by a mob because they were a Christian, what would you do?

NOW READ ACTS 21:27–36

Immerse

Paul has been travelling around much of the known world, preaching to whoever would listen – and that meant a whole lot of non-Jews. But he has not rejected his Jewish roots (although he has rejected the limited Jewish understanding of God's big plan of salvation). That's why he goes into the temple and takes part in religious rites (v 27). But the Jewish opposition is never far away. Paul is about to be killed when, in a dramatic turn of events, the Roman authorities pluck him to safety, because they want to maintain the peace! Who would have thought that help would come from that quarter? But then, God is a God of surprises. He answers prayer in ways that are far beyond our imaginations.

Re-engage

Christians in China have to be registered by the Chinese government and are only allowed to go to churches approved by the Chinese government – otherwise they're in danger of going to prison. If a Muslim in Saudi Arabia converts to Christianity, he or she could face the death penalty. Christians in North Korea get sent to concentration camps, where they are tortured and often killed. Christians in Burma have had their churches burnt down and have often had their children taken away and forced to become Buddhist monks. In Eritrea, government-sponsored gangs raid churches and burn Bibles.

>And this happens in dozens of countries, all over the world, wherever governments or majority religious groups feel threatened by Christians, sometimes because they're a threat and sometimes just because they're a bit different.

>If you do, thank God that you live in a country where Christians don't face persecution on that scale. Spend some time praying for Christians in countries where following Jesus could get you imprisoned, tortured, or murdered. As you pray, expect God to act in unimaginable, surprising ways.

>Want to know more? Check out www.csw.org.uk (Christian Solidarity Worldwide) to find out how Christians suffer.

Airlock: Heavenly

Themes: Evangelism, Courage

Truth at all odds

Decompress

What do you say if someone asks you what you do on a Sunday? Or what the Bible-study group you go to is about? Or what you think about religion? Would it be more or less difficult if this person was really aggressive towards you?

NOW READ ACTS 21:37 – 22:23

Immerse

It's really easy to get nervous. You don't know how people are going to react, and you don't want to cause trouble for yourself, and so you um and ah and skirt around the issue, or you lie, or you change the subject. Phew, you think. That was a close one.

>Paul's been arrested for a crime he has not committed, and he could have saved himself a lot of trouble by denying everything. But instead, he doesn't just come clean about the real reason he's in trouble, he also manages to tell his own faith story. On top of that, he confesses his own part in the murder of Stephen and points the finger at the culprits. (This part of the story is in Acts 7:1 – 8:1.) Bit of a virtuoso performance, really. It might not be the way to get people on your side, but it was the truth – Paul knew it was an opportunity to tell people about Jesus.

>But the final spark that re-ignites the anger of the crowd is his declaration that God intended non-Jews to hear about this message. Again and again, this is the point at which a sympathetic crowd turns on him!

Re-engage

We all get put in places where we get chances to say what we believe. What's more, if we are praying about opportunities to speak for Jesus, those opportunities are far more likely to come. In his first week at uni, Mark decided not to drink any alcohol. It wasn't that he didn't like the odd pint, nor that he was hard up but he wanted to say to people that he was prepared to be different and he didn't need the crutch of alcohol to get through that first disorientating week. He lost count of how many times people asked why he was prepared to be different, which was an open invitation for him to talk about his own faith story. And he was able to help a whole load of students who got hammered. Brave stuff, but he made a difference.

>Pray that God will give you courage this week to look for similar opportunities and the wisdom to say the right thing when the opportunities come.

Airlock: Heavenly

Themes: Wisdom, Strategy

You've got rights

Decompress

It can be easy to forget that we're living in a real world – we can spend so much time hanging around Christians and doing Christian stuff that it's all too easy to forget how the world works. Sometimes we miss out on things that we're actually entitled to. Does that ring any bells with you?

NOW READ ACTS 22:24 – 23:10

Immerse

Paul takes advantage of the rights he is entitled to, as a Roman citizen (and one who was born a citizen, too, which is a whole lot better than being someone who has bought citizenship). Does he know that this is the quickest way to get to Rome or does he simply do this to prevent his back being reduced to pulp? It was certainly a wise decision! God guided him. God's wisdom is called into service again when Paul confronts the council of the Jewish leaders. He energetically confronts the high priest but then offers some sort of apology. (His bad eyesight may have prevented him from recognising Ananias.) But then he introduces a contentious point of teaching which he knows will bring out all the animosity of the two factions in the council towards each other. Read verses 6–10 again. What a brilliant piece of verbal strategy and manipulation!

Re-engage

Christians as citizens or as members of a specific group are entitled to certain rights just like everyone else, but we do need to be aware of what exactly we are entitled to. Sometimes, we need to assert these rights (or the rights of others!) for the cause of the gospel and/or for our own preservation. (Incidentally, how aware are you of someone else's unjust treatment and any action you could take to change their circumstances – or do you go round with your head in the clouds, no earthly use at all?) On other occasions we need to do our homework so that we can strategically present the good news of Jesus or refute those who are hostile to it. We need God's wisdom if we are going to be able to do any of this. James wrote: 'If any of you needs wisdom, you should ask God for it. He is generous and enjoys giving to all people, so he will give you wisdom' (James 1:5). Get into the habit of chatting with God throughout the day, asking for his wisdom, especially when you know you'll be in a challenging situation.

Airlock: Heavenly

Themes: God's plan

Time-travelling

Decompress

Where do you want to be in a year's time? Do you know where God wants you to be? And what about your group of friends or your community?

NOW READ ACTS 23:11–22

Immerse

In today's Bible reading, Paul's in one of his tightest spots yet – his enemies, very devout Jews, are going to kill him, and they're literally not going to eat until they succeed. One person might be able to keep a secret, but 40?! The more people involved the harder it is to keep a secret, particularly when the bad guys have gone to the most important Jewish leaders and asked for their help. It probably isn't surprising that Paul's nephew hears about it, and it isn't a difficult decision for the young man to let Paul in on the secret. He then takes steps to spoil their plan.

>Paul knows he is going to Rome – God has told him so (v 11), so he knows that it isn't God's plan for him to die, just yet. And as it turns out, God does protect Paul. God does so through various stages. First, Paul's nephew finds out. Then he has the guts to go to Paul and then to tell the Roman commander. This commander takes the nephew seriously and dramatically removes Paul from the scene of danger – Paul is safe for the time being!

>The Bible doesn't tell us if the plotters actually starved themselves to death!

Re-engage

The point is, if God has a plan for you, he's going to make sure that his plan happens. What's more, his plan for one person is only part of a bigger plan which embraces lots of other people, and even whole nations. That was what was at stake for Paul. For the sake of the gospel, he needed to get to Rome. The challenge is often to know what the plan is, not just for us, but as part of the bigger picture. We're not generally quite as privileged as Paul in knowing what the future holds and that is probably a good thing. But ask God to give you an idea of what he plans for your group of friends or even your part of the world. You may be surprised what insight he gives you, especially if you do this with other people. And you will have a part to play in that! Now that really is time-travelling!

Airlock: Heavenly

Themes: **Authority, Honesty**

Spin doctor

Decompress

Have you ever got worked up when someone in the media has put a particular spin on a story so that they are seen in a good light, but you know that is only part of the story? Ever done that yourself, or has it ever happened to you?

NOW READ ACTS 23:23–35

Immerse

Paul, under the protection of Claudius Lysias, is spirited away, up the coast, away from Jerusalem. Actually, even if this happened at the dead of night, troop movements of this size can hardly happen silently. Just imagine the sound of 280 horses' hooves, let alone the trampling of 800 feet. But at least Paul is now safe. And Claudius Lysias, the commander, presents himself in a favourable light – the one who rescues Paul, the Roman citizen (single-handedly?), who is sure Paul is innocent (but is not prepared to release him) and has now discharged his responsibility to his senior! But for Paul this is part of God's plan for his life and he appears to accept it. After all, he is the man who can write these words to the Christians in Philippi: 'Christ gives me the strength to face anything' (Philippians 4:13, CEV).

Airlock: Heavenly

Re-engage

Christians are caught up in a world where people, including those in authority, lie and spin the truth. We should not be surprised at this, however hard it may be. We need to remember that Christians are those who are serving the God of all truth, who is above all lies and deceit. That doesn't make life any easier but we can discover for ourselves the truth of Paul's words to the Philippians. That's what Sam experienced when a gang of people in his class turned against him for no obvious reason and spread lies about him. Even the teachers believed them. Sam was devastated. It was so unfair. Salvation came when one teacher determined to get to the bottom of it all and at the end of the year arranged for Sam to be moved into a different class. Sam was much the stronger as a result of all this. Only later could he see that God had been with him and had given him the strength!

>Pray for anyone you know who is a victim of bullying or a campaign of lies. Pray too for those in authority who may be tempted to tilt the truth in their favour. It may not appear to matter initially but the long-term effects are often very significant.

Paul gets out of trouble with the help of people in authority – the Romans, who governed a large area of Asia and Europe. They're really people doing their jobs, for the most part. He knows that he hasn't broken any of their laws. (The Romans have not yet introduced the law that made Christianity illegal.) Paul knows that he has to respect their authority.

Authority can work on our side. We're supposed to be good citizens. It doesn't mean that we have to tolerate unjust laws, but it does mean that part of our Christian responsibility is to respect the people who make and enforce the law as people who are just doing their jobs. They are doing it for the good of others. What attitudes do people you know have towards those in authority – at school or college, police, local councillors, government, church leaders?

Extra 1_Romans 13:1–7
Extra 2_Matthew 22:15–22

Themes: Judgement, Hope

You've been warned!

Decompress

List ten words that describe God and then work out the opposites to those words. Being without God doesn't sound attractive when you put it like that, does it?

NOW READ ISAIAH 32:9–20

Immerse

Divide this passage into three sections (9–14, 15–18 and 19,20). The first describes how God's people were under serious threat from Assyria, the superpower of their day. Isaiah had a message from God that they were currently in the calm before the storm, and the invasion was going to happen within a year! There will be scenes of desolation: even the palace will be empty and the cities deserted.

>But there is hope! God's Spirit will be poured out and things will be better than before: deserts will be fertile places and the plants that grow will be enormous. It will be a time when God's people live in peace and justice. Isaiah has jumped from a literal, specific prediction of impending doom to metaphors of a better future – a new heaven and a new earth!

>The last two verses jump back to the nearer future: the forest and city in verse 19 represent Assyria's destruction, and are shown in contrast to a happy future for God's people: growing crops and tending animals.

Re-engage

The doom and destruction were coming because God's people had turned away from him. Isaiah was trying his best to warn them and get them to turn back, but his message was falling on deaf ears. God sometimes uses other people to speak to us – are we ready to listen to their advice, or, like God's people here, do we 'know better'? Sometimes if we won't listen he allows the bad consequences of our actions to bring us to our senses. We've been warned!

>The time of God's Spirit being poured out began at Pentecost (Acts 2), continues today and will conclude with God's new creation at the end of time. Look again at the characteristics of that era; is that fruit shown in your life? Go back to the list at the start and write out ten things that you would like God to improve in your life. Take some time and space to ask God to pour out his Spirit on you again to help you change.

Airlock: Heavenly

Themes: **Faith, Disaster**

God is in control

Decompress
Look out of the nearest window at the biggest object you can see. How does that compare to God?

NOW READ ISAIAH 33:1–13

Immerse
I imagine Isaiah looking out towards the advancing Assyrians one moment, then looking up at God the next. He does this three times in this passage. In verses 1, 4 and 7–9 he focuses on the Assyrians. The first verse could be summarised, 'those who live by the sword, die by the sword.' Verse 4 describes their plundering the land, and the last look at them describes how they take people into exile (they had already taken away the people in the north of Israel) and break peace treaties. All of this happened – look at 2 Kings 18,19.

>What faith Isaiah has to be able to look to God in the face of such an enemy! In the intervening verses Isaiah calls out for strength and salvation; he affirms that God is great (even if what's going on around him doesn't seem to confirm that); and he anticipates God's decisive action.

Re-engage
What things are going on in the world, or in your life, that seem to deny that God is in control? At times like this the devil will try to discourage us and suggest that there is no God, or that he doesn't care. This is one of his favourite questions that he uses to sow the seeds of doubt: 'How can a God of love allow this to happen?' The reality is that we may not get answers to all of those questions this side of heaven, but the way to respond to them is to affirm what we know to be true about God, just as Isaiah does.

>So what do you know to be true? If you are struggling, start by looking at what Jesus said and did. Jesus' life, death and resurrection are the perfect antidote to doubt – these things really did happen: historical documents verify many of them! So if Jesus lived, died and rose again, what sort of God do we trust?

Airlock: Heavenly

The future's bright...

Decompress

'I have good plans for you, not plans to hurt you. I will give you hope and a good future.'
Jeremiah 29:11

> How does this make you feel?

NOW READ ISAIAH 33:14–24

Immerse

Isaiah is a real visionary – he foresees a future in which God's people live in harmony with him and those who oppose him tremble. He is not describing the way things are now, but using a tense called 'the prophetic present' which uses the present tense to describe the future because the future is so certain with God that it might as well be happening now.

> This is anticipating the restoration of Jerusalem as the capital of God's people, but more importantly the restoration of God's people as those who live correctly. Their relationship with God is shown in their lifestyle: right actions and truthfulness; using their money correctly; refusal to think wrongly. Things will be so good then that the oppressors of the past will be a distant memory. In God's certain future there are no threats on the horizon, no diseases, and 'their sins (will be) forgiven.' It's a picture of bliss and harmony that the people will need to hold onto during the time of oppression.

> Notice the order of verse 22: an awareness of God's justice is shown by his law (which we can't keep). We need the king to come and sort out our failure to keep his standards (which he has done in Jesus).

Re-engage

For believers in Jesus, the future is certain and could be written in the prophetic present tense. He will be with us always by his Spirit. Our physical death is not the end, but we will be raised like Jesus to a new eternal life. We will get to see God face to face. Think of other things too and write them in the prophetic present. Stick these things around your room as encouragements to you during difficult times. Put some inside your Bible and diary so that you will come across them later on.

> Notice that the people of God here put their faith into action. Look again at verse 15. Does that describe you? Hopefully you aren't planning murder, but Jesus said that hating someone was the same as murdering them (Matthew 5:21,22)! What practical steps can you take to change your lifestyle to match this list?

Airlock: Heavenly

Theme: End of the world

The final countdown

Decompress
Read John 3:16. Who does God love? How much does he love?

NOW READ ISAIAH 34

Immerse
Run for cover! This is God's holy wrath unleashed in a terrible triumph. This is a message for the whole world, not just God's people in one small corner of the Near East. Here we have a picture of final divine judgement and eternal desolation. If ever the word 'apocalypse' was to be used correctly, it would be here. The land of Edom is used as an example of what will happen to all nations.

>This is a short-term warning for the nations of the Near East (the Babylonians were hot on the heels of the Assyrians). But there is a longer-term prophecy as well, which anticipates a time when God will finally say, 'Enough!' Those who have not said 'yes' to him will suffer the terrible consequences of their actions.

>This prophecy is written in poetic language that is not meant to be taken literally, but the key point is meant to be taken seriously: God is going to judge everyone, and it will be terrible for those who have opposed or ignored him. Look at verses 16 and 17. These things have been written down as God has inspired them. All these things will happen because God is in control. But we are left in suspense until chapter 35 for the really good news (cue *EastEnders* drums: dum, dum, de dum dum…).

Re-engage
This passage is one of those that inspire a sense of urgency about telling other people about Jesus. The future for those who do not follow him is bleak (putting it mildly). Remember John 3:16? God doesn't want anyone to perish, but will respect our choices, which have consequences. If we have said 'yes' to Jesus we do not need to be worried for ourselves. But like Isaiah we ought to warn others.

>If we use language like Isaiah today we will be dismissed as a crank. If we speak honestly and earnestly about how important our faith is to us, those who love us ought to listen. Think of one person you'd like to become a Christian. Start praying now for an opportunity to share your faith with them and that they will be responsive. Keep praying – remind yourself with a note placed somewhere you'll see it.

Airlock: Heavenly

Themes: Hope, Transformation

Optimism overload

Decompress

Imagine you are in a pitch-black room. Now imagine that you have lit a candle. The situation is transformed by a small light. How can God use you to transform a dark situation?

NOW READ ISAIAH 35

Immerse

These words would have seemed hollow to those people who were eventually deported (2 Kings 25). Yet they are words of incredible hope and optimism. Between Babylon and the land of Israel was a massive desert that no one could cross. To get back home they would have to go around it and it would have seemed impossible that it would ever happen, yet Isaiah's prophecy anticipates a miraculous return – on a road that went right through the desert. Again, the language is poetic, not literal, but the message of hope for God's people is in stark contrast to the message of doom for those who don't trust God (Isaiah 34).

>The images here are not of mere survival, but of total transformation. The apparently hopeless situation that God's people will find themselves in is not the end.

Re-engage

This chapter is followed by an account of Assyria's invasion of Judah, the southern part of what had once been Israel. It is preceded by a prophecy of doom and devastation. It is a beacon of hope in the face of overwhelming odds. Copy it out and put it somewhere you will remember it so that you can read it when you get despondent.

>Many people are forecasting the extinction of the Christian church in the UK in the next couple of decades. Attendance numbers are on the decrease and 1,000 young people leave church every week. What's the hope for the future? The hope is the same for us as it was for the people facing a bleak future in Isaiah's day. But the hope is not for the restoration of the church, it is for the lives that are transformed by God's Spirit. He can do the apparently impossible. He can do it for nations; he can do it for you. He can do it through you.

>You may think I'm suffering from optimism overload – I prefer to say that it is because I believe in a God who can transform desert places.

Airlock: Heavenly

Are you in need of comfort? Are you in need of knowing that God is in charge and that he will be with you through whatever is happening in your life?

Read Isaiah 35 again. It was written for the people of Judah, but could just as easily apply to you. Be sure of God's promises to you.

Extra 1_Revelation 21
Extra 2_Matthew 5:4

Theme: Truth

Don't believe the hype

Decompress

When people who work in banks are trained to spot fake notes, they aren't shown forged money for weeks. Instead they spend all their time with the real thing. They become so familiar with the true currency that when they see a dodgy note it stands out a mile.

NOW READ 2 CORINTHIANS 11:1–15

Immerse

We live in a society where we're constantly bombarded with messages. Whether it's advertising slogans on TV and billboards, magazines telling us we need to be thinner/browner/taller/lighter, or our friends saying, 'Come on, it won't matter if you just do it once.' With all this going round in our heads, it can be incredibly difficult to remember and hold on to what we know to be the truth. It was the same in Corinth. The Christians there were being bombarded with confusing messages from false teachers – something which has been happening since the beginning of the human race (v 3). There are some of these false teachers in churches today; you've probably seen reports of preachers abusing members of the congregation or preaching stuff which we know is wrong. They can often be very convincing, as can the other messages we get bombarded with from the media and society. We need to go back to the Bible to get the true message.

Re-engage

I don't wear a WWJD? (What Would Jesus Do?) bracelet, but I think the idea is a good one – always looking at Jesus for our example. There ought to be a WDBS? (What Does the Bible Say?) bracelet too, and my minister reckons there should be WDJD? (What Did Jesus Do?) as well. By looking to the Word of God and the Son of God, we get the truth. Going back to the illustration of the bank workers, the more we get to know God, the easier it is to spot what's not from him. The more in touch with the Bible we are, the easier it is to see when people are telling us stuff that's simply not true.

Airlock: Heavenly

Theme: Trials and tribulations

It's a hard knock life

Decompress

'Those who are treated badly for doing good are happy, because the kingdom of heaven belongs to them.'
Matthew 5:10
>Pray that today you'll really believe that living this Christian life is worth it. It's not easy, but it is worth it.

NOW READ 2 CORINTHIANS 11:16–33

Immerse

Don't ever let anyone tell you Christianity is for wimps. Just look at this incredible list of stuff Paul's been through for the sake of spreading the gospel – you could sell this to Hollywood as a blockbuster movie script! Prison, beatings, the death penalty, being stoned (not like that!), shipwrecks, getting mugged, being attacked by Jews and non-Jews alike, and ending up cold, hungry and tired. Added to all this physical hardship, he's also got the mental burden of constantly worrying about these young churches he's looking after (v 28). And you thought you had it hard! So why's he telling us this? Well, in the context of the previous warning about false teachers, he's saying, 'Look, this is the proof that I'm telling the truth. Why would I go through all this if I was a false prophet too?' He is rightfully boasting that he would sacrifice his life for his beliefs – something the false teachers would never do.

Re-engage

What this should also do is encourage us in our daily lives. God doesn't call all of us to undergo the severe hardships that Paul experienced. But as you well know, living the Christian life can be very, very tough indeed. Getting teased by friends; not having other young Christians around us; dealing with temptation; struggling with family problems, illness or bereavement. God gives us the strength, peace and patience to face up to our problems. Don't let your trials and tribulations get the better of you. Take them to where they belong; take them to the foot of the cross.

Airlock: Heavenly

Theme: **Strength**

The question of suffering

Decompress

We can't understand God. Otherwise he wouldn't be God. We aren't supposed to understand him. It's certainly healthy to question him, and when we do he'll answer us. But like with Paul here, it might not always be the answer we're looking for.

NOW READ 2 CORINTHIANS 12:1-10

Immerse

Almost everyone knows someone who's affected by cancer. My sister's best friend died from it. My uncle's dying from it. I know God does miracles, and I know that, for whatever reason, there are some people who get miraculously healed from these illnesses, and lots more who don't. I can't pretend to know the answer. But Paul here gives us a small insight into what it's like living with constant suffering. The thorn in his side is an illustration – it's thought he may have had malaria, epilepsy or a disease that affected his eyesight. Whatever it was, it wasn't easy for a man like Paul to live with. Like any of us would, he says, 'Why me Lord? Make it go away!' (v 8). But God doesn't work like that. God says in verse 9, 'My grace is enough for you. When you are weak, my power is made perfect in you.' That's a tough answer to prayer, but one that Paul accepts and gets on with.

Re-engage

I'm fortunate enough never to have suffered from any major illness or disease. But I have been in many situations where God has really worked through me because I was really down and out and having to rely completely on him. This passage is about suffering, but it's also about our attitude to serving God. When we are weak, he makes us strong (v 10). Paul talks a lot about boasting, trying to give God the glory for what he does through us, rather than taking credit for it ourselves. It's obviously something he struggled with, because he reckoned in verse 7 that God actually gave him his painful problem to make sure he got his priorities right. Are we trying to do it all ourselves? Is there something in the way of your relationship with God that you need to let go of so you can serve him better? Like Paul, we have to rely on God's strength, not our own.

Airlock: Heavenly

Theme: **Being taken for granted**

Don't be ungrateful

Decompress

An Athlete song starts 'You are loved, and you know you are...' That's how Paul feels towards his young Christians in Corinth. And that's how people feel about you. Don't forget it.

NOW READ 2 CORINTHIANS 12:11–21

Immerse

Ever feel taken for granted? It's not a nice feeling. My ex-girlfriend had a habit of doing it to me at times. You end up feeling a bit worthless, like they're taking advantage of you: it's all take and no give. And it sometimes happens at work: I'll slave for hours doing something, and often get no thanks or feedback. Sometimes you get a negative comment and you ask yourself 'Is this really worth it?' But the problem is, we do it to other people all the time. Ask any friend, parent, teacher, youth leader, minister. Paul is certainly feeling it here. What I like about his letters is that he's very human, and not afraid of saying how he feels and what he's thinking. He's fed up that he always has to prove himself to the church at Corinth; it seems nothing he does is good enough for them (vs 12,13). In verse 19, he says, 'Everything we do, we do it for you.' Here is a man totally committed to spreading God's word and building up the church. And what does he get in return? Read verses 20 and 21 again. How disappointed must he feel?

Re-engage

I've been working with young people in church youth groups for 11 years now. A lot of the time it's incredibly rewarding. But a lot of the time you do get taken for granted. I want you to think especially about your youth leaders/ministers etc. Are you taking them for granted? What could you do to encourage them? How can you show them that what they're doing is worthwhile? In verse 21, Paul says he is 'saddened' for the Christians he knows are doing the wrong things. That's a really strong term to use and shows how upsetting it can be when people you invest in disappoint you. Make sure you're not causing those people who love and care for you to grieve. Don't take them for granted.

Airlock: Heavenly

Theme: Examining your faith

Getting a check-up

Decompress

If you had a spiritual X-ray now, what would you be able to see on it? Would you be embarrassed if a doctor held it up and other people could see? Pray that today God will show the areas of your faith that need attention.

NOW READ 2 CORINTHIANS 13

Immerse

I recently ran the marathon. I had to do months of training and preparation. The race itself was mid-April; I started my training programme at the end of November. As a result of doing so much running I started getting problems with my knees which meant I had to see a physio. She told me I had various biomechanical problems and the only way to sort it out was to do cetain stretches. Each time I went she'd give me some new stretches to add to my workout. I ended up dreading the check-ups because it meant more work and more stretches for me. But doing those stretches every day was the only way to make my knees strong enough to get though the 26.2 miles. At the end of his letter here, Paul encourages his readers to get a spiritual check-up (v 5). You might not like what you find; there might be disciplines you need to take up to get your faith back to full fitness. There might also be things you need to cut out. Paul's worried about what he's going to find when he meets with the Corinthian Christians. If you're worried about your spiritual fitness, get back into training now. Don't wait to see a doctor or until you're really out of shape.

Re-engage

The thing that really impresses me about Paul in these passages is the way he relates to the Corinthian Christians. They're obviously struggling with a lot of issues (12:20,21). Paul could: a) be legalistic and lecture them on the laws they should be obeying; b) stop writing to them and turn his back on them because he doesn't want to deal with their problems; c) gossip about them and turn other people against them. But he chooses none of these. Instead he continues to build on his relationship with them – sharing, communicating and caring. We need to follow his example in the way we relate to people around us, both Christians and non-Christians.

Airlock: Heavenly

If we're not suffering/being persecuted, does that mean God isn't blessing us?

Extra 1 Philippians 1:27-30
Extra 2 Ephesians 6:10-20

Themes: **Respect, Marriage**

Sacking the Queen

Decompress

The Jews think of the story of Esther as a panto. They read it at the Festival of Purim, cheering the good guys and booing the bad. As the curtain rises on our pantomime, step back into the past with us to a land far, far away, where a king only had to give an order and it was so. And it came to pass that a great king gave an enormous banquet for his officials and nobles. Ask God to give you fresh insight into this rather extraordinary story.

NOW READ ESTHER 1

Immerse

At this banquet the King, called Xerxes, (pronounced zurck-sees) ordered his queen, called Vashti, to come to display her beauty to his friends. She said, 'No.'

>The trouble was if women in the land got wind of the fact that the queen had disobeyed her husband, then they might all start saying, 'No.' And that would be big trouble. Women's liberation was a while off. All the male officials wanted to do was preserve harmony and peace. Showing mutual respect between men and women was just not part of the scene, so we should not expect it to be in evidence!

>The queen got the sack, the men of the land were given more authority and everything probably got a bit harsher. Your disobedience almost always has consequences for somebody else. Also, sacking the queen created quite a large vacancy. How to fill it?

Re-engage

Today we don't force people to respect their husbands or wives, elders or betters. Does that make respect more valuable when it actually happens? Or should we have a social hierarchy? If and when you get married, how will you respect your partner? Will it depend on how much they respect you or will it be unconditional? Queen Vashti's lack of humility in realising her real position had devastating consequences for other people. Spend a while talking about these things to the one who always shows respect and rarely gets the respect he deserves.

Airlock: Heavenly

Themes: **Loyalty, Obedience**

Queen Idol

Decompress

Have you ever felt as though you don't matter that much to the people you know? How does that square up with what you know about God's opinion of you?

NOW READ ESTHER 2

Immerse

Welcome to the new elimination TV show, *Queen Idol*. And step forward Mordecai (pronounced more de kye) and his stepdaughter, or cousin, Esther (Hooray! – remember to cheer). All the most beautiful young women in the land are given a year's beauty treatments and then paraded before the king, who gets to pick the new queen. This might seem outrageous to us as a way of choosing a ruler's wife, although the audience-elimination exercises to find pop idols and relaunchable celebrities are not so very different.

>Notice Esther's attitude. She obeys her stepfather and, on entering the palace, sticks to his instructions. She doesn't take advantage of her surroundings to ask for luxuries but is content with whatever her supervisor suggests.

>This is how to win approval. Esther sets an example of getting on in life through taking advantage of opportunities yet accepting the limitations that come along with them. It might be a passage to read for all those who desire fame. But be careful!

>Esther wins the competition and becomes queen. What is more she is able to save the king's life when she hears of a plot to kill him. Coincidence? God-incidence?

Re-engage

Noticed anything strange? This is the Bible, right? No mention of God in the story so far though. Have you wondered what he's up to?

>In this story God works through the day-to-day coincidences and opportunities of life. Here is a Jewish man and a girl he has brought up who, in a very matter-of-fact way, make the most of an opportunity that arises. They must have known the stories of God's people in the past, the stories where God has a role for unlikely people, such as David the shepherd boy, Moses the refugee, Abraham the wealthy farmer. Are you ready to take everyday opportunities to be useful to God? Are you looking for them? Talk with God about this if you expect him to answer! It could be risky!

Airlock: Heavenly

Themes: The individual, Prejudice

The bad guy

Decompress

Dan joined the class in Year 9. Within a month the cheerfulness that characterised the class had changed into a competitive aggression. It was tough for Sam as a Christian in that class. Suddenly everyone was trying to be clever, intolerant and all that sort of thing. It was like that for the next five years. Sound familiar?

NOW READ ESTHER 3

Immerse

Enter the bad guy, Haman (remember to boo). He gets promoted, and in our panto wanders around the stage doing evil laughs and expecting everyone to bow down to him and worship him. What power! We are not told why Mordecai, a Jew, would refuse to bow down to Haman. Was it because, like Daniel, he would bow only to his God? Was it because he identified Haman with the previous plot against the king? Was it because he was just stubborn? Who knows?

>All we do know is that Haman decided to take it out, not just on Mordecai, but on all his people. Haman is described in verse 10 as 'the enemy' of the Jews. (Boo! Hiss!) Would Mordecai have done what he did if he had known that his actions might lead to the death of all his people? Haman's and Mordecai's individual actions are worth comparing.

Re-engage

In our society, we wonder if we can make a difference on our own. Most people just get submerged in the crowd. But the truth is that sometimes it only takes one person to stir up trouble in a previously tolerant, multi-cultural society.
>Alternatively, it can take only one person to inspire people to live in a more positive way!

>How tolerant are you? Do you want to make a difference, even if no one else is on your side? And how could you be sure that you were not a tyrant in the making? Talk with God about one of the issues of injustice you care about – for example, race, disability, age! What scope is there to change or worsen this situation and what are you doing about it?

Airlock: Heavenly

Themes: Loyalty, Courage

The good guy

Decompress

'All my life I have been waiting for a time such as this.' Ever heard anyone say that? Many people will say that once or twice in their lives there comes a time when all their gifts, skills and life experiences come together to achieve something. Have you said that yet? Esther's moment is coming up.

NOW READ ESTHER 4

Immerse

We're thinking of putting a sign on our office door saying, 'If you don't have an appointment expect to die unless it's really urgent.' We hope it will buy us a bit more uninterrupted peace! Even powerful kings of the ancient world did not want to be interrupted against their will.

>Big job for Esther (Hooray!) to do then. Pluck up courage and go see the king even though he tends to kill people who come to see him without an invitation – yes, even queens. The seriousness of the situation was all too clear to every Jew involved!

>So what does Esther do? She gets her people to fast (going without food, and praying instead). And she fasts herself, along with all her staff. She is remarkably composed, almost as though she had been preparing her speech in verse 16.

>In the Gospels, we find Jesus following this pattern: spending time with God before big decisions or momentous occasions. This was most notable at the very start of his ministry when he was without food for 40 days and was tempted in the desert (Luke 4:1–13), or when he faced his death in the garden (Luke 22:39–46).

>Note Esther's bravery in verse 16: 'If I die, then I die.' Notice too that the roles had reversed. In 2:20 Esther did what Mordecai said. In 4:17 he did what she said! They were in this together!

Re-engage

If you are troubled and facing a major, even a deeply significant choice or dilemma, why not think about praying, fasting, weeping (it really does help express what you feel and even discover emotional release!), wailing (have a good shout), sackcloth (wearing uncomfortable clothes to remind you that you are in an uncomfortable state), ashes (marking your forehead with ash – a sign that you are praying for something).

Airlock: Heavenly

Themes: **Humility, Impatience**

The plot thickens

Decompress

Now it's been a while since they had a banquet and Esther knows the way to get to a man's heart is through his stomach. So she makes the king a nosh-up. OK, we expect her servants did it, but you get the point. Esther is in no rush. Have you ever been really desperate to make something happen but know you've got to bide your time, just wait a bit longer? Patience is hard, especially in a tense situation.

NOW READ ESTHER 5

Immerse

Esther uses all her charm to get an audience with the king. Touching the tip of the king's sceptre (a sort of staff) was a gesture of humility. It was an acknowledgement that he had the power over her life, held in his hands.

>She throws a banquet for the king and Haman. (Still booing? Good.) She uses it to invite them to another one. Meanwhile, Haman (Hoo! Biss!) is getting uptight that Mordecai keeps refusing to do the bowing and respecting thing. He also boasts that he has been to one meal with the king and queen and has been invited to another one. He is in a real rush to get his reward.

>Haman's wife suggests building a ridiculously high gallows (a tower to hang people from) and asking the king if he'd mind awfully having Mordecai hung form it. Well if you get to eat with the king regularly why not ask him for a favour or two yourself?

Re-engage

Note the contrast between Esther's approach the king and the way Haman mouths off that he has been invited to a royal nosh-up. Contrast his haste with Esther's calm actions.

>Some characters in the Bible had to wait an awfully long time for the moment when they acted significantly for God. Take Abraham, who was 100 when his promised son arrived; or Moses, who was 80 before he led the people of Israel; or Paul, who spent three years in Arabia and Damascus preparing for his journeys to preach the gospel; or Jesus himself, who was 30 before he began his short ministry on earth!

>How impatient are you to be doing things for God rather than getting to know him and his ways so that you are ready when the right time comes? Now there's something to talk over with God!

Airlock: Heavenly

Extra H/31–35

LOOK OUT!! BEHIND YOU!!

What's your favourite panto? *Mother Goose*? *Babes in the Wood*? *Macbeth*? (Oh, come on! All those ghosts and witches? It's crying out for someone to start shouting, 'Behind you!')

Although some treat the story of Esther like this, there is a lot more to it than just being a good story. Think about some of the stories from the Bible that you know and love. Why are they so great? Are they just 'good stories'? Often these great narratives can teach us much more about God than we ever imagine.

Extra 1_Daniel 1–6
Extra 2_Philemon

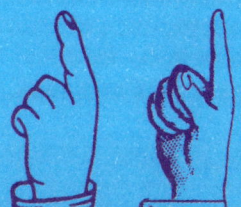

Theme: **Evangelism**

Get out of jail free!

Decompress

What's the strangest opportunity you've had to tell people about Jesus? Did you take it? What happened?

NOW READ ACTS 24

Immerse

Paul's genius is knowing the right time and the right way to say what he believes. It's also quite possible to bring matters of faith into the conversation at the wrong time. Part of the reason Paul knows he has to speak out when he does is because he knows that being a Christian is the real reason he's in prison in the first place. The accusation of stirring up trouble is only an excuse to get rid of him.

>Success is never guaranteed! Felix, the Roman governor, talks to Paul endlessly, maybe because he is genuinely fascinated or more likely because he is after a bribe (v 26). One friend from a county where corruption and bribery are very common said that this is one of the key passages in the Bible which indicates the wrongness of accepting bribes. It is really important for Christians to have grasped the significance of what Paul has chosen to do. He could easily have raised the money to get out of jail! And everyone knew this. But he refuses to act in this way. He always wants to act with integrity and honesty. However, he certainly uses the opportunities that he has over the next two years! That's a long time when you could have got out of jail *almost* free!

Re-engage

That's one of the great things about Paul. He knows when to speak and exactly how to present his argument to a specific audience. But he also behaves in a way that marks him out as someone who is prepared to be different, someone who strives to be honest and not squeeze himself into the mould of this world's values.

>Spend a bit of time praying that you'll know the right time to tell people what you believe and that you'll have the courage to say it. Pray too that you will be willing to behave in ways that are different, that mark you out! That could mean your attitude to money, leisure activities, relationships, sexual activity, ambitions! You can no doubt identify other issues too! It's worth talking with your Christian group about what it means to be different and how that affects others.

Airlock: Heavenly

Themes: **Perseverance, Freedom**

Trapped?

Decompress

How often do you give up when things go wrong? What is it that stops you giving up? Or what is the final straw?

NOW READ ACTS 25:1–12

Immerse

It's easy to fall into a state of utter despair. You face a minor setback, or a really big one, actually, and you get it into your head that there's no way out, and that's it – depression, misery, defeat.

>You'd think that Paul would do the same – he's got no hope of release; the Roman governor, Festus, wants to get Paul's enemies on his side; and a whole gang of important Jewish elders want to kill him. Things are looking pretty bad.

>So what does Paul do? He thinks big. He might never have the chance to be free again, but he's going to use his position as an important political prisoner to make sure that he's at least going to be able to spread his message to the single most important human being on the planet at that time – the emperor. So he uses his right as a Roman citizen to get his case referred to the emperor's court.

>He might not be free, humanly speaking, but he's going to a place far away from his enemies, and he's going to have a chance to speak to the emperor himself. That's thinking big! He has chosen to serve the King of kings. That is true freedom.

Re-engage

We may feel trapped and unable to see our way out. But in times like these, God's love peeps through. There might not be a way out of every situation, but that doesn't mean that God can't use it in some way. Sometimes the chance of using it is obvious; sometimes it isn't obvious at all; and sometimes it's so obscure that you might never see it without God's help.

>Some difficulties help us learn more about God or about ourselves. Some difficulties allow us to show people how God's love works in our lives, and some give us a chance to tell more people about Jesus.

>Going through a hard time? Take a hard look at it. God can remove the barriers that make you feel trapped or depressed. Or he may simply be with you in that, helping you to keep going. If you are serving the Kings of kings, doesn't that make a difference?

Airlock: Heavenly

Theme: Communication

From the outside

Decompress

Ever talked with someone and realised that they had views and experiences which affected how they 'heard' what you were saying?

NOW READ ACTS 25:13-27

Immerse

King Agrippa's great-grandad was the Herod who was visited by the wise men at Jesus' birth. His family, who were Jewish, had ruled in Judea for years and at the same time had maintained an uneasy relationship with their Roman masters. His dad (called Agrippa too) had actually been brought up in Rome, well-connected with the imperial family. This King Agrippa now sort of ruled parts of Judea. One of the few powers he had was to appoint the Jewish high priests.

>So here he is, with Paul – a Jewish leader (who cosies up to the Roman authorities) meeting a Jew who is a Roman citizen (who refuses to cosy up to the Jewish authorities, or the Roman ones for that matter!). What a confrontation!

>But Paul's interrogators are both weak men – we don't hear about Bernice's part in all this. Festus cannot make his mind up. Here he is, a powerful Roman governor who cannot work out what the charge is against a man whom every Jew in the land appears to want dead! So he consults a visiting, weak, but self-promoting Jewish 'king' – see verse 23. What qualifications do these men have to pass judgement on the truths that Paul is explaining? What attitudes do they have?

Re-engage

A recent television series put Christian expectations of teenage sexual activity under the microscope. It was done in a thought-provoking way without concealing the Christian convictions of those running the project. It had a mixed reception from the media. Some reporters were positive but one critic was furious at what he perceived as manipulation of the young people. How dare Christians act in such a controlling way? It was a valid comment and it is good to be aware of how Christians come across. But on the other hand we might ask how far this critic understood what he was judging.

>Ask God to give you insight into the attitudes and expectations of those who will hear you explain what your faith means to you. They may not be convinced but your insights may help you to avoid making inappropriate statements.

Airlock: Heavenly

Theme: Conviction

Strong feelings

Decompress

What do you feel strongly about? The success of your football team? The most recent album of your favourite band? The selfishness of your brother or sister? How easy is it to convince anyone to agree with you by strong words or discussion?

NOW READ ACTS 26:1–24

Immerse

Paul addresses Agrippa directly and tailors what he says to Agrippa's own understanding. He speaks clearly and logically. He rightly assumes Agrippa knows much about Jewish faith and practice. He speaks of his own experience with utter conviction. Agrippa is quite detached, while Festus makes a puzzled and angry outburst. He thinks Paul is nuts! Discussions have been going on for months and months and have failed to make sense to Festus.

> I am sure Paul had not wanted all parties to remain unconvinced of what he passionately knew to be the truth. But, as he knew all too well, arguments on their own will not convince anyone to become a follower of Jesus. The Spirit needs to intervene, however calmly or dramatically. As John wrote: 'The Spirit will show them (the people of this world) that they are wrong about sin, because they didn't have faith in me' (John 16:9, CEV).

Re-engage

Can you recall any discussions about what you believe that you've had with friends or other people at school or college? How heated have the discussions been? Have you presented Jesus in a calm way that has made sense or have you got carried away? (Of course, it does help to be a bit passionate – then, at least, people know that this really, really matters to you.)

> Jane and Bex had been friends since Year 7. Jane had shared her Christian faith over the years, sometimes with lots of strong feeling. At the end of the Sixth Form, the two of them went away together. As they set off, Bex said, 'Jane, can you tell me about what you believe? I need to get this sorted out before uni.' Why had she never asked this question before?

> Ask God to help you explain him clearly to your friends and also to trust in his Spirit to help people understand! And don't get discouraged if people tell you you're crazy. It's a normal human reaction, and frankly, if God wasn't behind it, it would be crazy. But God can do the impossible.

Airlock: Heavenly

Theme: **Tough decisions**

The hard way

Decompress

Have you ever been faced with an easy and a hard way out of a situation? Which did you take?

NOW READ ACTS 26:25–32

Immerse

Paul is set on going to Rome, and he knows that it's God's plan for him to get there. He also knows that it's going to cause him a lot of difficulty and pain. He could have been released, and he probably would have been able to tell loads of people about Jesus if he was on the streets again. But this wasn't the way it went. He appealed to the emperor himself, so he had to go to Rome.

>I think that Paul knew he could have been freed if he hadn't appealed to the emperor, and I think he knew that he wasn't going to get out alive, but he also knew that he had to be faithful to God's plan.

>And this meant that he had to go about things the hard way. On the other hand, he also knew that God was going to protect him every step of the way.

Re-engage

Sometimes the best way to do something is not the easy way. Take dieting, for example. You can lose a shedload of weight by simply not eating anything but lettuce for a couple weeks. You'll get thin pretty quickly. However, your health might suffer and the moment you start eating normally again, all that weight will fly back on.

>Actually, there are two secret foolproof rules for losing weight and getting rid of that flab for good. Come closer – I'm only going to say this once. Eat healthily and exercise more.

>'But wait,' you say, 'that's too much like hard work! Why can't I just go on one of those faddish diets?' There's nothing stopping you from doing that, but those sorts of diet aren't much good for you, and don't keep your weight down once you stop them. The only way to keep trim and healthy is to eat healthily, and exercise. Which takes a whole lot longer and is a lot more work.

>Is there something in your life that you need to achieve, something that you know is the right thing to do? Are you going about it the hard way or the easy way? Talk honestly with God about the choice before you.

Airlock: Heavenly

Extra H/36–40

Sometimes it takes a bit of time for God's plans for your life to start working out. The waiting can be really, really painful. Paul sat there under house arrest for over two years, while he waited for the Romans to get their act together. He never gave up, and never lost sight of God's plans for him.

Centuries earlier, the people of Israel, in exile in Babylon, were reminded by the prophet Jeremiah of God's plans for them. The fulfilment of those plans was far from easy. Find out what God had planned for them.

Extra 1_Jeremiah 29:11–14
Extra 2_1 Samuel 16,18,24,31

Themes: Justice, Punishment

Three steps to heaven?

Decompress

'Dear Lord, help me get it right. It's simple, but so difficult for me to put into practice. I pray that you will help me see through your word what it is that can keep me straight on your path.'

NOW READ MICAH 6

Immerse

You've all seen the court scenes of great trials on the TV. Many TV dramas have, over the years, featured at least one episode involving the rights and wrongs of the main characters. It is the way dramas look at the moral validity of their stories, and not surprising that moral dilemmas crop up all the time. And it is not just in the dramas that these things are explored: the legal system is also often in the news, be it the trial of a celebrity, the fall of a ruthless dictator or the end of the road for an evil criminal. And three millennia ago it wasn't much different.

>Although following a similar theme to the previous five chapters of Micah, things take a decidedly dodgy turn for God's people. Now they are hauled into the courtroom, but they face a scene like no other. Again the imagery here is fantastic. Take a moment to reflect on the jury. Not Chris Figis from down the road doing his two weeks service for Queen and country. No, it's the mountains! And why the mountains? Because they are almost eternal in their being, unlike humans who come and go in the twinkling of an eye.

>And what is the case being brought? God has been so good to his people and yet they have turned away from him. He saved them from Egypt and brought them into this land, but they have been wicked. Ahab and Omri are two of the kings being pointed out here, but it wasn't just shoddy leadership, it was the whole nation. And they couldn't even claim ignorance, for they had been told time and time again how they should live.

Re-engage

There is little to add here. This 'Re-engage' section should give you some pointers in taking what you've just read into your walk with God. So why is there little to add? Well, quite simply, the basic structure can be lifted directly from the Bible text. Micah 6:8 gives a wonderful summary of how someone who follows God should live, and so in summary, as you put down *Airlock* for the day, go forth and act justly, love mercy and walk humbly with your God. Amen.

Airlock: Heavenly

Themes: **Anger, Mercy**

How can I stay angry?

Decompress

Take a moment to think about the community where you live. Is it a town, a city, a village? Are you stuck in the middle of nowhere? Is it so crowded that you feel you have little room to breathe? Well this is your culture, your society. What holds it all together?

NOW READ MICAH 7

Immerse

The basic idea of civilisation, of society, is that as a group of people we have decided to live together and follow some basic rules. In democracies we elect the leaders, but throughout history there have been other forms of leadership and government. In this final chapter we are given an image of that civilisation breaking down. Rulers, judges, neighbours (not the Ramsey-Street kind), friends, even lovers and relations become divided and break down: society falls apart. This is the fate of a God-less people of God.

>And yet that isn't the end. There is a glimmer of hope. Micah is watching and waiting for his God and Saviour to sort things out. Despite the fact that Judah will go into exile, God has shown him a time when the nation will once again rise.

Airlock: Heavenly

>In the film *Spider-man* we have the line 'with great power comes great responsibility'. Well, if this chapter had a similar line it would be 'with great anger, there comes great mercy'. Because the nation has turned from him, God will turn from them. But because God loves his people he will also show his mercy and restore them, and through that restoration we know that Jesus shows the greatest act of mercy of all time.

Re-engage

Christianity in the West is in a bit of a crisis: numbers attending churches are in decline and it seems that divisions within the church are causing split after split. We don't know where the church will be in the future, but if Micah has shown us anything it is that God will not leave us alone. However small in number we may become, he will not stay angry or leave us forever. With confidence we can cry out to God and ask him to do great things.

>'Dear Lord, help us stay focused on you, love you and follow you, and keep our eyes set firmly on you. Lord, we cry out for you to do great things. We know that you love us and ask that you would show us continued mercy as we live following you. Amen.'

Themes: **Judgement**

'Vengeance is mine!'

Decompress

'Dear Lord, please help me understand these words, spoken so long ago to a specific group of people about specific events. Please help me see that they can mean something to me as well.'

NOW READ NAHUM 1

Immerse

This is a specific prophecy from the Old Testament. The words refer to the destruction of Nineveh, the Assyrian capital. This happened in 612 BC. Seeing that the words of Nahum do not have a go at Judah for not following God's ways, we can also probably say that this prophecy was made a short while after the reforms of Josiah in 621 BC (read about him in 2 Kings).

>From the book of Jonah we know that the Jews weren't too keen on the Assyrians and from the history books we also know that they were a ruthless empire when at war. If there had been international war crimes trials back then, Assyria would always have been in the dock.

>After a quick description of who Nahum is (doesn't really tell us too much, does it?) this chapter starts by stating God's credentials. Why can Nahum give this prophecy from God about Nineveh? The bottom line is that God is good, he loves his people and those who stand against his people, though victorious in some battles, will ultimately lose the war.

Re-engage

This is almost like God's CV; there is a lot in here that we can hold onto into times of trouble and distress. Just look at verse 7. If you ever needed a verse to copy out and stick up, then you can't go far wrong with that one.

>Jonah was asked to tell the people of Nineveh that this powerful God would destroy them if they didn't change their ways, if they didn't put God first. Do we have a message to take to those who don't put God first? Do you need to make sure where God is in your life?

>Spend some time praying for God's guidance as you tell others about him. He is a God of love, but love is not weak.

Airlock: Heavenly

Theme: God's sovereignty

How the mighty fall

Decompress

'Dear Lord, give me a sense of how you have moved through history, guiding people to do your will, to bring about the downfall of those who do evil and granting wisdom for those who have brought good. Give me the strength to follow your will as you continue to be with us today.'

NOW READ NAHUM 2

Immerse

From historical records outside of the Bible we know that Nineveh was destroyed in 612 BC, and the city was razed to the ground. But in the years before those events, Nineveh, and the Assyrian Empire, was crumbling.

>In an almost satirical attack, Nahum mocks the once great city, calling on it to try and protect itself. But that will all be in vain. The city and all it stood for will be destroyed. The epicentre of the evil empire will fall, all its wealth carried away to other lands.

>If this chapter tells us one thing it is that no one can stand against God. We've got superheroes coming out of our ears in Hollywood, but most of them have a weakness, something an enemy can use to try and defeat them. But not God. Verse 13 gives us a statement of fact, 'I am against you,' and with those words, the city of Nineveh and the Assyrian Empire had no hope.

Re-engage

No one can stand against God. Take a moment to think about what that means. Nineveh was the epitome of evil in its day. It doesn't take a long look at our world to see its modern day equivalents. How could God use you to shout out against the evil in the world today?

>It is a wrong assumption to see prophecy as merely predicting the future. It is speaking forth God's word. For Nahum, speaking God's word was delivering the message of judgement to Nineveh. For us it may be something different. We need to listen carefully to God so that we can speak his word into the evil structures that we live in today. Nineveh may no longer be standing, but evil has plenty of energy left in its legs, and so the world needs more Nahums. Fancy the job?

Airlock: Heavenly

Themes: **Sin, Judgement**

Go ahead, make my day

Decompress

Decompress
'Dear Lord, help me to play my part in your fight against evil, as you bring peace where there is war, love where there is hate and joy where there is sadness.'

NOW READ NAHUM 3

Immerse

I laugh in the face of people who say that the Bible is irrelevant; I tweak the nose of people who think that it is out of date and of no use to their lives! (That's enough Blackadder references – Ed.) OK, what I'm on about is this passage. The theme of evil that runs through this chapter is unbelievably similar to the type of thing that goes on today.

>As we've seen, Nineveh is a bad place (can you see now why Jonah didn't want to go there?) and here we see the complete corruption of Nineveh explained. Take a moment to go through the list of things that Nineveh and the Assyrians get up to and see how relevant they are to our world today. See? The Assyrians were a warlike nation and they were led by desire, by greed. The imagery used here likens the Assyrians to a prostitute, a simile often used in the Bible. Here it relates to the way Assyria attracted other nations into her snare, deceived them and then took them for all they had.

>But as with all evil, God stands against it and although that means destruction for Nineveh it also means hope for God's people.

Re-engage

The cruelty of the Assyrians is similar to the cruelty that we see in our world today: evil is still around! But God still stands firm against it. When Nineveh finally fell, it was at the hands of other nations – ordinary people carried out God's plans.

>So how will God deal with the evil in our world? Ultimately everything will be sorted at the end of time; but until then, it is through ordinary people that God continues to work out his plans. And by ordinary people I mean you and me! We can take on the fight against injustice, oppression, unfair trade rules and so on. For with God on our side we too can make a difference to the world; we too can overcome the evil that is still around; we too can bring peace where there is war, love where there is hate and joy where there is sadness. Amen!

Airlock: Heavenly

When I was at university, there was a woman who would stand outside the cinema, the Students' Union, indeed anywhere where there would be a lot of people, and hand out tracts and talk to people about Jesus. Most people thought she was mad, including me (especially as she told me off for going to see a film, 'What would Jesus think if he came back and found you in the cinema?' 'Erm… I think he already knows I'm here…'). Most people laughed at her.

It may not have been the best way of doing it (some of her preaching followed the line of Nahum's message in chapter 1); but at least she was challenging people about what they were doing. She was trying to call people back to God, to be holy and devoted to him.

How do you react to people in the street preaching the end is nigh? Do they embarrass you? Why? Do you think they have a positive influence on people?

Extra 1_Luke 4:16–30
Extra 2_Acts 9:19b–30

Themes: Words, Justice, Love

I'll take sticks and stones

Decompress

How would your friends describe you? How would your enemies describe you? How would God describe you? Which description is easier to believe? Which description is true?

NOW READ PSALM 64

Immerse

I don't know why but parents/guardians/teachers/random puppets on kids' TV shows still all insist on teaching children the rhyme, 'Sticks and stones may break my bones but words will never hurt me.' We all know it's not true. Words can seriously hurt, whether they're insults and abuse from strangers, tactless comments from friends or nasty lies being spread about you.

>David, the author of this psalm, had seen more than his fair share of sticks and stones from people trying to hurt and kill him. But even he, the king, a pretty popular and decent guy in his time, someone we're supposed to look up to as being a good example, even he still worried about what people were saying about him behind his back. The key bit is that David took his worries to God. He voiced his complaints because he knew God cared; and more importantly, he knew God could do something about it.

Re-engage

The thing about nasty words is that they often come back to haunt the people who said them. Lies and rumours spread about innocent people only make the liars looks stupid when the truth comes out, and those who insult others are likely to attract the same kind of feelings in return. God does sort things out in the end, which is a comforting thought if you have been on the receiving end, but also something to think about yourself when talking about others.

>But that's not the end of it. The scars that words can make can cut deep, even if we've seen our attackers get what they deserve. Think back to the questions in 'Decompress'. David went to God when he heard what people were saying, because he knew that ultimately, what matters most is what God says. Do you know what God says about you in the Bible? Try looking up Romans 5:8, Psalm 139 or Ephesians 2:10. Remember them, and next time other people's words get you down, God's Word – the truth – can be your refuge.

Airlock: Heavenly

Themes: Faithfulness, Prayer

Gonna be a sunshiny day

Decompress

Do you have a 'to pray for' list, whether it's in your prayer diary, church notice list or just in your head? What do you want to bring before God today? What answers do you hope for? Do you believe those answers will come?

NOW READ PSALM 65

Immerse

Prayer is a funny thing. Sometimes it can feel like we've got to keep praying for the same thing for ages, perhaps forever, before we see God doing anything. Sometimes it can feel like we've got to keep praying for the same thing over and over again just to make sure God doesn't forget to keep on doing something.

>But every morning, the sun still comes up. Some days you can't see it because of the clouds, but it's there and we'd notice if it wasn't. It's not just plants that rely on sunlight to live.

>While we're worrying about whether God's going to look after our pets while we're on holiday or if he'll ever tell us whether we should be a car mechanic or a chiropodist when we're older, God's sorting out the basics. He does it day after day without fail. Funny how it's easier to trust God to keep the oxygen from spinning off out into space like he has been doing every day for thousands of years, than it is to trust him that he's got that important decision next week sorted out for us.

Re-engage

In the psalm, David is pretty confident about how God answers prayers. The first sentence says that God can expect us to fulfil our end of the bargains, in return for the promises he always keeps.

>Quite a few challenges for us there. Can we pray expecting God to answer us? To keep having faith that God is working even if we can't see it? Can we sit back and trust God to sort it out?

>Have a think back to what's been on your 'to pray for' list in the past, and why some of it's not on the current version. Is there anything that has been answered that you need to thank God for? It can be easy to forget promises made, 'God if you just help me now I'll…' Maybe it's time to remember to keep your end of the deal? If you don't have one already, starting a prayer diary or noticeboard might help you keep track.

Airlock: Heavenly

Themes: **Thankfulness, Praise**

Thanksgiving day

Decompress

What do you have to be thankful for? Are there any things that you're not so thankful to God for? Are there any things that you know you should be thankful for, but you forget about and take for granted?

NOW READ PSALM 66

Immerse

When God does so much stuff for us, day after day, saying a quick 'thank-you' prayer can sometimes seem repetitive and meaningless. When God does such amazing miraculously big things for us, 'thank you' doesn't really express what we want to say. When God does things we don't really understand, and we end up wondering why on earth he's making us go through it, we don't even want to say 'thank you' at all.

>Yet, this psalm thanks God for all of those things. It's easy to remember to thank God for the big things he does for us, but not always easy to know how to. It's not so easy to thank God when we're going through hard times, but we should, because God works through times like those to change us into the people he wants us to be. The hard times also teach us to be grateful for the little things God always does for us. The fact that he's with us all the time, he loves us and he hears and answers our prayers, the things we can take for granted and forget to thank him for.

Re-engage

So how should we thank God? How can we praise him like the psalm tells us to? Praise is more than just a quick 'thank-you' prayer. We can sing songs of praise to God, but praise is also more than a nice uplifting song. We can shout praise to God, but your friends might find that a bit weird if you start doing it on the bus in the morning.

>Would your friends find it strange if you started telling them all about the cool thing that happened to you the other day? Everyone loves to tell others when something great happens. Why not when God does something great for you? We don't have miraculous escapes from Egyptians, but if you can show them something that's visibly changed in your life, that's real praise. If you can show hope and trust in God through hard times, that's real praise to God.

>Now, you can use all those spare 'thank-you' prayers to remember the stuff he does for us all the time, and to remember exactly why God deserves to be praised with our lives all the time.

Airlock: Heavenly

Themes: **Action, Evangelism**

Heaven is a place on earth

Decompress
Do you know anyone who needs God in their lives? Can you think of any situations in the world that need God in them? Does the rest of the world really need God or are we best keeping him to ourselves to avoid offence or awkwardness?

NOW READ PSALM 67

Immerse
It doesn't seem very politically correct to expect people all over the world, from different cultures and different religions, to praise our God. Aren't we supposed to tolerate others' beliefs and that? Live and let live seems to be the politest way, and often the easiest too.

>But do you ever wonder what the world would be like if everyone was a Christian? Terrible for music fans probably, but just think: that person you know who's always horrible – maybe they'd be a bit nicer, or at least try to be. That person you know who's always quiet and on their own – maybe they'd be a bit happier. On a larger scale, would the wars stop? Would people learn to share and stop hunger? Or at the very least, would the people in trouble have the strength to go through it if they knew God was with them? We wouldn't all be perfect, but at least we'd be trying. I guess we won't really know until heaven...

Re-engage
Still not encouraged to get out there spreading the word? Well it might be awkward and it's definitely something to approach tactfully; but really, we have a responsibility to get this worldwide praise thing happening. All those things we've been thinking about that God does for us... they're not for us at all. The whole point is to show God at work, so everyone can see how good he is and want to praise him and know him.

>So if we just sit there accepting the blessings and doing nothing, it's all going to waste. Not only are we supposed to tell other people about the great things God does for us, but we're supposed to share them as well. Actually do them for other people. People may not like preaching but they always like a bit of no-strings-attached free stuff. Spread the love, spread the cash, spread the prayers and the cares and anything else you can think of. What has God provided you with recently that you can give away? What has God done for you that you know someone else needs as well?

Airlock: Heavenly

Themes: **Prayer, The Bible**

Life, the universe...

Decompress

Are you sitting comfortably? It's a long one today, but full of pretty much all we ever need to know. Including whatever it is that God knows you need to hear today. Sit back, and listen out for the answer!

NOW READ PSALM 68

Immerse

The Hitch-Hiker's Guide to the Galaxy, or any other travel book for that matter, is full of good stuff about how to get by on your travels around the universe, or Thailand or the tube. There are many books around with various philosophies and self-help plans that aim to help us get by in life too, but none tell us everything we need to know – or the book publishing companies would go out of business.

>At least they would do if anyone twigged that the Bible has already done that. The words and the pages might not seem big enough to hold the secrets of the universe, but when God himself speaks through them, we can learn everything we ever need to know.

>This psalm kind of covers it all: God protecting us; what he's done for us in the past and what he'll do for us in the future; how we should respond with praise and why. Because this psalm above all shows how God rules over the entire earth, not just those who follow him.

Re-engage

Maybe there's a bit of this psalm that really jumped out at you today, or a bit that described or answered something you were already thinking about. If not, then verses 19 and 20 are a good place to start. The Bible is a big book and some of it (you know the bits) might seem a bit irrelevant, but all together it tells us that God is our Saviour; he wants to help us in life and save us from death.

>Just as it would be silly to go on holiday and feel lost because you didn't bother to read the guide, if there are clues to how life works, what God is like, and what's going to happen in the future, doesn't it make sense to find out?

>It's a classic question but, face to face with God, who knows everything, what questions would you ask? Well, you *can* ask him whenever you like. The answers may not come booming out of the sky in a deep voice, but God can speak to us in many ways: through the Bible, through other people, through the things around us. Ask him your question now, and listen carefully for the rest of the day.

Airlock: Heavenly

'Search and you shall find...'
Luke 11:5–13

Still not hearing from God? Not convinced that he's got an answer, or that he's even hearing you in the first place?

If you're looking for an answer in the Bible, rather than just flipping open the book and reading whatever page you land on, subject guides or topic indexes in the back (or front) of your Bible can help. If you don't have either of those, try a Bible search engine on the web (www.biblegateway.com is a good place to start).

Extra 1_2 Timothy 3:10–17
Extra 2_Deuteronomy 6

Theme: **Faith**

No heed to Hear'Say

Decompress

'When the Son of Man comes, it will be like what happened during Noah's time.'
Matthew 24:37

NOW READ MATTHEW 27:32–44

Immerse

Having endured the bullying of the guards, Jesus is now subjected to the 'tutting brigade' of Jerusalem.

>You can imagine the gossiping old ladies: 'Ooh, I always said he would come to no good – mixing with all the riff-raff…'

>And the sarcastic businessmen: 'Come on then – you told me my riches were no use in heaven, but at least they'd have got you a decent lawyer.'

>And the snidey religious leaders: 'Oh dear – have your magic powers failed you? I thought you were supposed to be the Son of God – so save yourself.'

>All the people at the crucifixion seem so far away from God's plan, and we may think we would behave differently, but we have the benefit of the hindsight of the resurrection.

>I wonder where the disciples were. Perhaps they were already in hiding – fearing for their lives and wondering whether the amazing Jesus' journey was all over.

>The problem was that no one could think in God's ways – and even today no one can. But guess what? That didn't matter to God – his plans were above all human thoughts. The Jews may not have thought they needed saving, but God was going to do it anyway…

Re-engage

It's amazing how changeable people are. One week, they're shouting, 'Hosanna!' and the next week it's back to, 'Who are ya?' For Jesus, it was the equivalent of the Hear'Say phenomenon.

>But all those psalmists and prophets who said that people were like sheep were so right. We don't think for ourselves; we follow the crowd and back whoever look like they might win.

>Human nature loves to see someone fall. It makes us feel better about ourselves, looking down on someone else's mistakes. But Jesus didn't watch people fall down past him and leave them there. It didn't matter who the person was that fell, or what they had done. Luke gives an interesting account of the criminals whom Matthew mentions; it's well worth a read to see how Jesus continued to practise what he preached, even when he was left alone himself…

Airlock: Heavenly

Theme: **God with us**

Strength in weakness

Decompress

'After walking a little farther away from them, Jesus fell to the ground and prayed, "My Father, if it is possible, do not give me this cup of suffering. But do what you you want, not want I want."'
Matthew 26:39

NOW READ MATTHEW 27:45–56

Immerse

If you were on the heavenly church council, the chances are that you would not choose for your leader's last words to be 'My God, my God, why have you rejected me?'

>Luke and John have a much gentler version of Jesus' last words, that portray Jesus as a faithful hero to the last moment. But I really rather like this version. So often we forget that Jesus was a man; a human capable of feeling all the emotions and fears that we feel. Sometimes it seems like Jesus was a kind of Julie Andrews character that could magic away any doubts through his super-holy powers.

>But, there would have been no point to Jesus' life if he didn't fully experience being human. And being human meant experiencing all the fears of the cross – had it really all been worth it?

>This is a moment of Jesus in weakness. But the difference between Jesus and the other people that we have met is that Jesus did not let his weakness stop him from doing what he was sent for. And guess what? God knew that as well. He knew Jesus would be obedient right up to his death, and that was how God planned to defeat the enemy once and for all.

Re-engage

There have been times in my life where I have felt the same way as Jesus – wondering why God has forsaken me in a time of need. Usually it has been my own fault, but sometimes life seems totally unfair, and everyone seems to have abandoned me.

>Yet notice how in the passage God has not forsaken Jesus at all. At the moment of Jesus' death, God makes his anger totally clear with heavenly pyrotechnics.

>Now I'm not saying that you should expect earthquakes and grave-breaking when you're in trouble, but God's light is most visible in the complete darkness.

>God has promised that in times of sorrow, he will comfort us, and in times of weakness, he will uphold us. He may do this through many different ways, but God will never forsake us – even in death: that is the promise of the cross.

Airlock: Heavenly

Theme: Generosity

Turning the tide

Decompress

'The group of believers were united in their hearts and spirit. All those in the group acted as though their private property belonged to everyone in the group. In fact, they shared everything.'
Acts 4:32

NOW READ MATTHEW 27:57–66

Immerse

It is difficult to imagine how it must have felt for the two Marys. To have seen Jesus cheered by a huge procession of followers on the Sunday, and then crucified to the jeers of the same people by Friday.

>And yet the tide is beginning to turn. Joseph of Arimathea uses his influence on 'Putty Pilate' to take Jesus' body and give it a decent burial. In fact, it seems that Joseph buried Jesus in the tomb that he had been making for his own death. Whether or not Joseph expected Jesus to break out of the same tomb within three days is an entirely different matter…

>Of course, the Jews are still running scared – what if the disciples run off with the body and claim that Jesus has been resurrected? So they also go and make their case to Pilate, who gives the impression of being sick of the whole affair by now.

>And so Jesus is buried with the soldiers guarding the tomb against the disciples, and the women watching over the tomb presumably against the guards. The disciples are still conspicuous by their absence here, but Jesus is no longer alone – and he's all ready to use the women's faithfulness in the next phase of God's plan…

Re-engage

We often read about how difficult it is for rich people to be useful in the kingdom – something about passing wind through the eye of the camel (or something like that). But here is an example of a rich man using his power responsibly.

>Joseph took a risk by burying Jesus – it would hardly have gone down well with the Romans or the Jewish leaders, but Joseph had enough clout to get away with this. Notice how he uses the grave that he carved himself – only the best was good enough for Jesus.

>It can sometimes be difficult for us in a privileged part of the world to read passages about the pitfalls of being rich, but here's a positive example of how we should behave. Riches are a gift from God and they should be used to his glory, because (believe it or not), they're part of his plan as well!

Airlock: Heavenly

Theme: Faith

Don't shoot the messengers

Decompress

'Listen, my dear brothers and sisters! God chose the poor in the world to be rich with faith and to receive the kingdom God promised to those who love him.' James 2:5

NOW READ MATTHEW 28:1–10

Immerse

Isn't it amazing how quickly the disciples forgot Jesus' prophecy? As we saw yesterday, even the Pharisees remembered Jesus saying that he would rise again on the third day, but on that third morning… no one to witness Jesus' triumphant resurrection.

>Well, that's how the Jews would have seen it, because in those days, the witness of a woman counted for nothing. Women were to be seen and not heard, both in the temple and in public. And yet it was the women who remained faithful to Jesus, keeping watch at the tomb and tending to his body.

>Of course, Jesus could have appeared to anyone – Peter, Pilate, Herod, the Pharisees… All of these options could have taken the story in a completely different direction. Why did he rely on two women?

>Here lies the key to Jesus' ministry. It is not fame, or power or wealth that enables someone to do Jesus' work. It is a childlike, simplistic faith. Notice how the women do not question the angel or Jesus; they obey the words immediately. (Strangely enough, it is the disciples who have the 'faith' problems when they finally meet the risen Jesus.) God knew exactly the right people for the job, even though it defied human wisdom.

Re-engage

This story of the women's faith makes me realise how far I fall short of their obedience. If the angel had come to me with his message, I imagine I might have tried to justify or explain away what was going on.

>'So you're an angel? Right… How do I know I'm not dreaming? Is it really sensible for the disciples to be wandering around when there's a search warrant out for them? Couldn't Jesus just go straight to them? Have we got enough sandwiches and matching crockery for the picnic hamper?'

>Sometimes I am full of my own earthly intelligence, forgetting that God's wisdom is far above my own, and is able to deal much more effectively with the practicalities than I can. I pray that we will learn to trust God's plan, even when it seems downright stupid.

Airlock: Heavenly

Theme: Evangelism

Mission accomplished?

Decompress

'My dear friends, you have always obeyed God when I was with you. It is even more important that you obey now while I am away from you. Keep on working to complete your salvation with fear and trembling, because God is working in you to help you want to do and be able to do what pleases him.'
Philippians 2:12,13

NOW READ MATTHEW 28:11–20

Immerse

The final words of Jesus to his disciples are important to Christians both today and through history. They encapsulate our reason for living, and they are like the 'quick start' guide to Christian living.

>Our aim as Christians is to spread the good news – that people have been saved from the evil in the world and there is a new life available to anyone who accepts what Jesus has done. The greatest words come right at the end: 'and I will be with you always, even until the end of this age.'

>Have you noticed how the opportunities arise for you to talk to people about Jesus when you least expect them? They may not be every day, but Jesus is there, nudging you into action and giving you opportunities to obey his final command. It's not a quick-fix job, and it will take time, but Jesus wants us to keep persevering with the job that he died for us to do.

Re-engage

This passage is sometimes a case of being easier said than done. But I want you to think for a moment about the state of the church when Jesus gave these commands. According to Matthew, Jesus was giving his commands to 11 men. And how many Christians are there now in the world?

>The greatest joy about reading this passage is knowing that Jesus' command has already been fulfilled through the ages: news of Jesus has spread through nations, through rich and poor, and finally to you and me.

>Of course, it's not over yet. There are billions of people who still need to hear and believe the message, and that's where we come in. But don't be afraid that Jesus' command doesn't work, because we can see through history that, to quote an advert for a well-known wood varnish, it does exactly what it says on the tin…

Airlock: Heavenly

Living for the Father

Alone in the darkness,
'Guilty' is my plea,
Condemned to death, unworthy,
I have lived my life for me.
I have broken the commandments,
I have disobeyed God's Word,
I have sacrificed the covenant
To proclaim myself as Lord.

Alone in the darkness,
A stranger they hanged,
Innocent and guiltless
He stretched out his hand.
He cried for the nations,
He pleaded for their lives,
Then he rose to death, victorious
And his soul's in paradise.

So is it true? Am I set free?
They say you break
    the prisoner's chains,
Did you even die for me?
My clothes are torn,
    with blood they're stained,
Yet you've given me
    your princely robes
And you've said you'll
    hide my shame.

Now I'm living for the Father,
I have glimpsed the face of God,
You have given me
    a second chance:
Servant to the servant-Lord,
I will live a life that's pleasing,
Turn away from my old sin,
And you've said that
    when I'm weary,
I can always turn to Him.

So is it true? Am I set free?
They say you break
    the prisoner's chains,
Did you even die for me?
My clothes are torn,
    with blood they're stained,
Yet you've given me
    your princely robes
And you've said you'll
    hide my shame.

Nothing I can do
    will separate me from you,
Nothing I can say
    will make you turn away,
You have broken the chains,
nothing will bind me again,
You have died for me,
    you've set the prisoner free.

© James Lovelock 1998

Extra 1_Acts 1–4
Extra 2_Romans 5:12–21

Themes: **Arrogance, Justice**

Turning the tables

Decompress

We all love a happy ending. (Hooray! Hooray!) But just before we get there, pause to think about the king. What impression have you got of him over these last days? A decisive leader, a just man, an intelligent man, someone you admire, ineffective? We are not given a very good impression of him at all.

NOW READ ESTHER 6

Immerse

Not exactly the usual cure for insomnia! The king gets out his favourite literature to while away the night hours – the chronicles of his own reign, his list of achievements, all the things he had done! Arrogant so-and-so.

>And as he read he discovered, instead of falling asleep, that he had missed out on rewarding Mordecai for saving his life. This spurs him into action. So he abandons the arrogance and thinks about being nice.

>Poor old Haman. He is wandering around the palace at night, even prepared to disturb the king's sleep in order to get the hanging under way. He hears the king's question, 'What should I do for someone I want to honour?' He assumes it is about him. Arrogant people always assume they are the ones we are talking about when we say good things.

>So Haman ends up being the one who parades Mordecai through the streets praising his name. Haman is totally ashamed. Try to imagine the depth of his humiliation! Then he remembers he has to go to the next banquet.

Re-engage

Even though there has been little about God so far in this story, there is a sense of natural justice in this tale. The humble are lifted up; the arrogant brought down to their knees.

>Mary said as much in Luke 1:52 when she heard the news that she would be the mother of Jesus. Read the words of her song and think about the topsy-turvy nature of the way God works! How much are you on the side of the humanly successful, the powerful, the strong? Do you define success, power and strength in the way that our celebrity-rich world does? Put into your own words how God sees these things. Talk with him about it.

Airlock: Heavenly

> Themes: **Grudges, Justice**

Comeuppance

Decompress

Esther's party for the king and Haman gets under way and is well into day two. This woman is good at biding her time. But just remember that Haman's anger has been boiling for quite some time. How long have you been harbouring a grudge against someone, or really letting someone get to you? Ask God to help you review your attitudes in the light of Haman and Esther.

NOW READ ESTHER 7

Immerse

Haman has had to lead his sworn enemy round the city telling everyone how great he is. Now he has to endure a two-day party where he is outed for being an enemy of the queen's own people.

>The king is so mad at this he has to go for a walk round the garden. Have you ever had to do that? It helps, unless you live on the 37th floor.

>Meanwhile Haman throws himself upon the queen's mercy, misses and lands too close to the sofa. The king comes back in with expert comic timing and thinks the queen is being molested. Before King Xerxes has a chance to do anything a servant mentions that there just happens to be an enormous gallows outside. How convenient. Haman gets hanged on his own tower. (Hip, hip, hooray!)

>The king calms down. Revenge is not a particularly clever idea unless you happen to be the most powerful person in the whole land and are sure you will go on for ever. For everyone else it's more trouble than it's worth. Jesus said an eye for an eye and a tooth for a tooth was no longer the best way (Matthew 5:38–42), however powerful you happened to be.

Re-engage

So read what Jesus said in Matthew 5:38–42 and think how differently Haman might have behaved. Of course, he was living before Jesus came to live and teach a new way of understanding the law and pleasing God. And of course, Haman did not love and serve the living God. But the attitude that does not seek revenge is so very different from the norm today! Think back to what you read of Mary's song in the last reading. Who makes you mad or has wronged you? What would Jesus want you to do?

Airlock: Heavenly

Themes: **Involvement, Justice**

Putting things right

Decompress

All very well hanging the ringleader, but what now? The law that Jews could be harmed still stood and the king's laws could not be cancelled. Time for some quick thinking, which luckily Mordecai and Esther have been quite good at so far. And Mordecai is put in charge of Haman's property. Can you think of any times when God used a few people to influence secular authorities to bring about good, and even the protection of his own people?

NOW READ ESTHER 8

Immerse

If you can't get rid of a law allowing Jews to be attacked, then write another one allowing them to defend themselves. Sounds weird to us but the people would have understood what this meant. Anyone even thinking of attacking Jews made themselves a target.

>Notice too that the attempt to get rid of the Jews led to there being more Jews (v 17). People reckoned that if being Jewish put you in favour with the king then being Jewish was for them. It sounds a bit like what happened when the Roman Emperor Constantine embraced Christianity and there was a wide turning to Christian faith. Much of that must have been genuine, but not all. And the history of the church in relation to the state has been affected ever since.

Re-engage

God still uses individuals and groups of individuals to bring about change in society in relation to big issues such as the abolition of slavery or the emancipation of women. Have you ever cared enough about something to bring about change? Do you care enough to exercise your vote at elections? If you are not old enough, it is never too early to care and get involved. Pray now about developing countries where pressure groups are making a difference, such as Iraq or Lebanon. Pray that the pressure groups will make a difference for the good and that God's activity will be evident!

Airlock: Heavenly

Theme: Celebration

Party time

Decompress

The Old Testament can seem to be a very violent place to us. Enemies are not locked up or exiled, but mercilessly killed. It is not just the Old Testament. History is gruesome. What are the significant incidents in world affairs that have happened in just your lifetime? How many of them were gruesome? How easy is it to remember?

NOW READ ESTHER 9

Immerse

It is not clear how the balance of power was changed by the king's latest edict. The clue may have been in the previous chapter – that many chose to be Jews rather than be slaughtered. It may just have been the psychological boost that the king's authority carried with it.

>Whatever, the Jews dished out hard punishment on their enemies and, in what can only be seen as barbaric tragedy, slaughtered 75,000 people (v 16).

>This has been a story to explain a festival, which may be why so many parties and feasts crop up in it. If you haven't noticed, just look back to check up! Many of the decisions taken in the story have been taken by drawing lots – *pur*. Mordecai and Esther initiated the feast of Purim which involves two days of partying and of gift-giving, especially to the poor. Their deliverance was so significant that it had to be remembered. And their intention has indeed been realised. The Jewish festival takes places even today, around March, one month before Passover.

Re-engage

But what do you remember of your faith journey? What has God done for you and in you? How do you remember? Every 27 January, Robert is given a bowl of daffodil bulbs as a sign of his new spiritual life when he finally gave in and accepted Jesus as his personal Saviour. That decision happened on 27 January 1975. Louisa has a tape of her baptism service that she plays every now and again. When Mark's spiritual mentor moved to another church, he gave Mark a book as a token of what they had learnt together. What do you do? At the very least, every time you participate in Holy Communion you remember Jesus' death and resurrection, until his coming again! Be thankful!

Airlock: Heavenly

Themes: God's kindness, Reward

Closing ceremony

Decompress

So what will be written on your tombstone? Through the many coincidences of this story Mordecai comes to be remembered as... Well read the last, short chapter and find out.

NOW READ ESTHER 10

Immerse

Verse 3 carries this tribute to Mordecai: he was held in high esteem; he worked for the good of his people; and he spoke up for the welfare of the Jews.

>Mordecai and Esther stood up for their God even when things got tough, and they emerged triumphant. The fact is that they were rewarded, but that was not guaranteed. Esther had agreed to approach the king even though it might cost her her life. Mordecai refused to bow to Haman at great personal risk. They wanted to be faithful to God. That was what mattered.

>We recall the words of the three guys in the book of Daniel about to be thrown into the fiery furnace for refusing to bow to other Gods: 'God ... is able to save us ... But even if (he) does not ... we will not serve your gods' (Daniel 3:17,18).

>On this occasion it all ended happily ever after, but that wasn't guaranteed.

Re-engage

Think through the story of Esther as it comes to an end. She has been humble, obedient, willing and courageous. Great things to be able to say about her. What will they say about you?

>And how important is it to you to receive a human reward as well as (or even instead of?) a divine one? Picture yourself standing now before God. Tell him how much you love him. (Be truthful. You cannot hide from him!) Praise him for all that you want to thank him for. Confess to him anything you know is standing between you. And now listen to his words of acceptance and forgiveness and the pleasure he takes in having you as his child Paul the apostle wrote: 'Now God has us where he wants us, with all the time in this world and the next to shower grace and kindness upon us in Christ Jesus' (Ephesians 2:7, *The Message* © 1993, 1994, 1995, 1996, 2000, 2001, 2002. Used by permission of NavPress Publishing Group).

Airlock: Heavenly

Extra H/56–60

There is little mention of God in the book of Esther (OK, there's no mention of God at all), but that doesn't mean he wasn't there. Look back at the whole story now, and you'll notice the extraordinary sequence of events that kept Esther, Mordecai and the Jews safe from the man who was trying to destroy them. God was working in the background, giving wisdom to those who needed it, using people's strengths (and weaknesses) to bring about his plan.

But we shouldn't be surprised! The Bible is full of people whose lives bear the stamp of God's faithfulness. Samson, David, Peter, Paul and many others all knew God's faithfulness, despite getting it wrong on so many occasions.

What about you? If you look back at your life so far, can you see God in action in your life? It might be good to do this with a couple of friends; you can share stories of God's faithfulness with each other.

Extra 1_2 Corinthians 11:16–33
Extra 2_Judges 13–16

Themes: **Advice, Discernment**

Shoot the messenger

Decompress

Do you usually take advice? Who from? Why? How good are you at telling people things they might not want to hear?

NOW READ ACTS 27:1–12

Immerse

It's funny how optimistic people can be! Whenever I get lost, I carry on regardless. I have no clue where I'm going, but I am happy to blunder about, sure that I will eventually find where I'm going to. I don't listen to anyone else, because then I would lose the satisfaction of finding my destination using only my finely tuned sense of direction. (I spend a lot of time doing this…)

>The men on the ship do this too. It was well known in Paul's time that you didn't sail anywhere in the winter – it was just too dangerous. But the captain and crew decide that they would risk it, despite Paul telling them that they'd get in trouble. Luke has spent a lot of time in the chapter saying how difficult the journey had been so far, but the captain doesn't seem to have learnt from this recent experience of tough sailing. He seems to ignore the fact that it would only get worse, because he doesn't like the harbour they are in.

Re-engage

Sometimes, as Christians, we have to be like Paul in this passage. We may have to tell people things they don't want to hear, and often we get a really hard time for that. But through all things, God is with us, and God helps us get through times like that. And it's up to us Christians to be there when the inevitable happens, and to get alongside people, and help them to pick up the pieces, without ever once saying, 'I told you so.'

>Sometimes, we're like the captain and crew of the ship – unwilling to listen to advice for any kind of reason. We've got to be prepared to listen to what people say to us. Not all of the things you hear are going to be pleasant. We've got to think hard about what we hear, and be ready to seriously think about whether it's right or not

Airlock: Heavenly

Themes: God's plan, Reassurance

Don't panic! Part I

Decompress
What keeps you going in the hard times?

NOW READ ACTS 27:13–38

Immerse
This is a really exciting story (unless, of course, you were actually involved; then it must have been pant-wettingly terrifying). The drama builds well – the wind picks up, ropes are tied round the ship to stop it falling apart, cargo is thrown overboard, clouds covered the sky for days on end, men try to escape but are stopped just in time – but while all this is going on, Paul is in the centre of it all, calmly telling people that they would all survive, but everything else would be lost.

>Paul's composure is extraordinary – I would be running around the ship screaming and generally embarrassing myself! But, of course, he has had a visit from an angel, letting him know that God's plan is still in effect, and that no amount of trouble at sea will change it. So, with this reassurance that he will still stand before Caesar to have his case heard, Paul sets about saving the ship, telling the captain that people were trying to escape, getting people to eat and preparing everyone for what was going to happen next.

>God's reassurance at a key time freed Paul to act the way he did, saving 276 people in the process.

Re-engage
Now, we might not be involved in a shipwreck (even if I was convinced I would be after watching *The Poseidon Adventure* when I was younger), but there will still be tough times in our lives, when it would be easier to abandon all hope and surrender to complete panic. But, while we might not have it direct from an angel that God is still in control, we should cling on to the promise that God has us in his grip and his plan is still in action.

>Gladys Aylward was a woman who knew that. God called her to go as a missionary to China, but all the missionary societies turned her down. Confident in God's plan, she decided to go there alone. All through her life, she faced hardship and danger – war, starvation, wolves, a Siberian winter and much more – but still carried on with God's plan for her life.

>Pray now, on your own or with a few friends, and ask God for reassurance that he is in control, even when things get tough.

Airlock: Heavenly

Themes: God's plan, Danger

Don't panic! Part II

Decompress

'(Jesus') followers went to him and woke him, saying, "Lord, save us! We will drown!" Jesus answered, "Why are you afraid? You don't have enough faith?"'
Matthew 8:25,26

NOW READ ACTS 27:39–44

Immerse

The sailors on Paul's ship were hardened sea-dogs – they knew how to sail a ship, and they'd probably been in trouble before. But in such a dire situation, it seems people forget all their experience and panic. Having already tried to escape on the lifeboat, leaving everyone else to die, the sailors take the first chance they get to make a mad dash for safety. Seeing the shore, they try and sail for it, but only end up stranding the ship on a sandbank.

>They are not alone in their panic: the soldiers want to kill all the prisoners so they won't escape (bit extreme). But God doesn't let that happen. He is still working out his plan for Paul, this time using the people around him. We have already heard that Julius, the army captain, was good to Paul (27:3), and now he steps in to save Paul's life. God has been preparing the ground, going ahead of Paul to make sure that no harm comes to him, to make sure that he arrives in Rome. And while this may seem another unnecessary diversion for Paul, God uses it to great advantage. He has already given Paul the chance to tell the people on the ship about him, and now more opportunities are just about to open up…

Re-engage

The contrast between the panic of the sailors and soldiers and Paul's calm assurance is stark, as was the difference between Jesus and the disciples during the storm on the lake. Paul has faith in God's power to save him, but the others don't.

>Having the same faith when things press in on us in our lives doesn't seem so easy. We easily start to panic, like the soldiers and sailors on the ship, and don't listen to what God is saying to us. It's almost as if the noise and terror of the storms of our problems drown out God's voice of reassurance.

>What storms are threatening to shipwreck you at the moment? Take some time out, maybe talk and pray through some of the things with someone you trust. Ask God for the faith to know that he is in charge.

Airlock: Heavenly

Themes: **Protection, God's plan**

Snake-handling

Decompress

Is there any situation in which you can't depend on God's protection?

NOW READ ACTS 28:1-15

Immerse

The thing about Paul is that he wasn't going out of his way to get into danger. He wasn't putting himself in harm's way. It wasn't his fault the snake bit him. And what's more, the snake biting Paul had a point to it. (Well, technically, it had two points, but what I mean is that there was a point to what happened, and not to the snake. If you get me.)

>The point was that God was protecting Paul. God's plan was for Paul to get safely to Rome, and this meant that he was going to get there. And also, it happened to show the shipwrecked sailors and passengers that he was special (they got the wrong end of the stick about it, but that wasn't Paul's fault).

>Anyway, the important thing is that Paul was just following God in everything, and making sure he followed God's plan. The snake-biting incident opened up many doors for Paul. He was able to show God's power by healing people, and no doubt he spoke about in whose name he was doing all of this healing. Shipwreck, snake-biting – God brought Paul through these life-threatening things to bring his message to more and more people. And then he finally makes it to Rome!

Re-engage

If you are going through the mill at the moment, this might seem a difficult question to answer, but what good things do you think God can bring forward from tough times in your life? Paul was able to use his life-threatening experiences to witness to people. Today, there are many people who can use hard times in their life to witness to the people around them. A friend of mine was suffering from MND (motor neurone disease), a terminal illness that affects the body, not the brain. As he deteriorated more and more, God used him to speak to those around him about Jesus in a very powerful way, not letting his disease stop him.

>If you are going through tough times at the moment, pray about them, and ask others to pray for you. But take some time to listen too. God might be saying that he wants to use you to do great things for him, even though you're feeling bad.

Airlock: Heavenly

Theme: Fulfilment

Journey's end

Decompress
Where do you want to be in ten years' time?

NOW READ ACTS 28:16–31

Immerse
Paul has finally reached the end of his journey: the great city of Rome. God has been preparing him to stand before the emperor and speak his word to the most powerful man in the world, and now he's finally there.

>Paul wastes no time in telling people about the good news of Jesus Christ. He talks to the Jewish leaders in Rome, and they listen quite openly. But after a while, when the time comes for them to decide if they believe Paul or not, we see the typical response to the gospel. Some people believe, but some people argue and refuse to listen to any more.

>Ever since his conversion on the road to Damascus, Paul has spoken bravely and often without regard for his own safety, confident in the knowledge that he is doing what God wanted him to. We're not really sure what happened to Paul after this – but it is fairly certain that he was arrested and executed in around AD 64 or 65.

Re-engage
What are our goals? What do we intend to do? Where do we want to end up? A lot of us have no idea where we're going. A lot of us have no idea what we want to do. And you know what? That's OK. It's all right not knowing your final destination, as long as you're following Jesus.

>Even if you don't know where you're going to end up, chances are that if you've been listening to God, you'll know when you get there; and the chances are that when you've been there for a while, you might need to move on. There aren't any hard or fast rules to this. Everybody's journey is different, and everybody has a different job to do. Your job is to go through, with God's help, listening as best you can, until you've got to your final goal.

>Think: when you've reached the end of the line, will you stick with it?

Airlock: Heavenly

...ke we keep saying: God's got a
...an for everyone who follows him.

...at's all very well, but how exactly
...es that work out? How do we
...ow?

...ere's no easy answer to that
...uestion. God tells some people in
...ry clear ways what they should
...e doing for the rest of their lives.
...thers, he tells just a bit at a time.
...e deals with each of us in a way
...e knows we'll cope with. Paul had
...uite a clear idea of God's long-
...rm plan, but others in the Bible
...nly saw little bits at a time. We just
...ave to keep praying and keep
...elieving, and we've got to have
...ith to know that God's plan is
...hat is right for us.

...xtra 1_Romans 8:31–39
...xtra 2_Hebrews 11